THE
SHAPE
OF
LOVE

THE
SHAPE
OF
LOVE

MASARU EMOTO

Translated by Noriko Hosoyamada

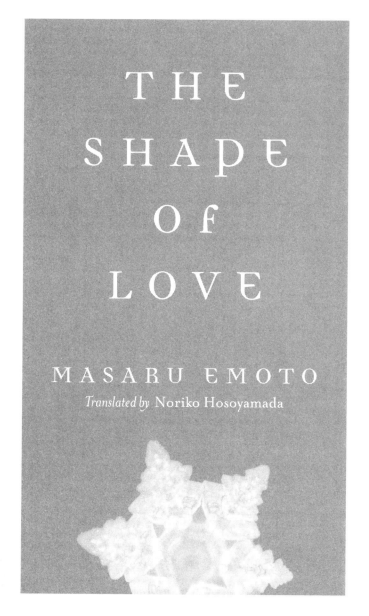

DOUBLEDAY

New York   London   Toronto   Sydney   Auckland

PUBLISHED BY DOUBLEDAY

Copyright © 2007 by Masaru Emoto

All Rights Reserved

Originally published in Japan as *The Shapes of Love in Water* by
Tokuma Shoten Publishing Co., Ltd., Tokyo, in 2003.
This edition published by arrangement with
Tokuma Shoten Publishing Co., Ltd.

Published in the United States by Doubleday, an imprint of
The Doubleday Broadway Publishing Group,
a division of Random House, Inc., New York.
www.doubleday.com

DOUBLEDAY and the portrayal of an anchor with a dolphin are
registered trademarks of Random House, Inc.

All photographs courtesy of the author

Book design by Mauna Eichener and Lee Fukui

LIBRARY OF CONGRESS CATALOGING-IN-PUBLICATION DATA

Emoto, Masaru, 1943–
[Mizu ga tsutaeru ai no katachi. English]
The shape of love / Masaru Emoto ; translated by Noriko
Hosoyamada — 1st ed.
p. cm.
1. Water—Philosophy. 2. Water—Psychological aspects.
3. Love—Philosophy. I. Title.
RA591.5.E45513 2007
613.2'87—dc22
2006034028

ISBN 978-0-385-51837-6

PRINTED IN THE UNITED STATES OF AMERICA

1 3 5 7 9 10 8 6 4 2

FIRST U.S. EDITION

CONTENTS

PREFACE

My first book on water, *Messages from Water,* was published in June 1999, and new readers continue to discover it year after year. In fact, it has been (or is in the process of being) translated into fourteen languages. My later title *The Hidden Messages in Water* was a collection of water crystal photographs; in that book I kept verbal explanations to a minimum so as to encourage readers to explore their own interpretations and sensibilities. It worked. The book spread by word of mouth throughout the world, like widening rings on water.

The Hidden Messages in Water was also intended to be a collection of messages about how to live: the messages I had learned from water through my research on *hado* (magnetic resonance) and water over fifteen years. With that purpose in mind, the book included many of my thoughts and inspirations.

The Hidden Messages in Water made the best-seller list in Japan and many other countries, and that success gave me courage and confidence. The book ended as follows: "When my soul is ready to set out on its journey to the cosmos, I fully intend to call out to everyone and say 'We're off to see the universe! Let's go to Mars!'" The widespread acceptance of my books encouraged me to pursue what I had wanted to write on for some time—that is, my thoughts on the eternal themes of human beings: Where did we come from? Why are we here? Where will we go after we die?

At the same time, Ms. Yumiko Toyoshima of the Tokuma Shoten Publishing Company really wanted me to write a book on the subject. But I hesitated because the number of requests for my seminars was rapidly increasing, and I was also already committed to some other writing projects. Furthermore, this book had a very tight schedule, giving me little time to write on these lofty, eternal themes. But Ms. Toyoshima's enthusiasm eventually made me agree to undertake this book, despite my extremely busy schedule. That was in the early summer of 2003. In the end, by twice confining myself to a hotel room, I managed to finish writing.

The reader may find shortcomings, but this book was meant to convey my thoughts on this subject. I believe that these themes by their very nature require all human beings to think about them on their own. It will be a great pleasure for me to hear criticisms and opinions from readers.

I must acknowledge the efforts of Ms. Toyoshima of Tokuma Shoten, who oversaw the entire publishing process of this book in Japanese. I thank her for putting it into such a wonderful form.

Masaru Emoto
September 2003

One

THE
SHAPES
OF
LOVE
IN
WATER

HOPE

There is an expression, "The heart is filled up with hope."

The water crystal depicted in Figure I might bring to mind an image of a child's chest filled with hope; his or her dreams are growing and growing. Note how the tips of the crystal seem to be growing farther out and the beautiful hexagon at its core. To have hope, people need a solid base, such as the one seen in this photograph. The source of the base is paternal and maternal love and education. In looking back at my life, I realize my mother's love enabled me to continue to hope to become a man who could contribute to world peace. I am grateful for her plentiful love.

Figure 1. The tips of this crystal seem to be growing farther out, just like the image of the word. Let us be the source of hope for others.

I was the youngest of four children, and I received my mother's full attention. My brothers did very well at school. Because I was the youngest child, not too much was expected of me. So I was brought up without many restrictions. After I married, my wife became the the bulwark of my life, just as my mother had been. Both my mother and my wife are like a big ocean that surrounds me in a relaxing way and lets me swim freely. I am grateful to these two women for enabling me to think that I can help build a unified world.

I hope that women who become mothers develop great love within themselves. Perhaps those who fully received maternal love in childhood find it easier to warmly love their children when they become mothers.

More and more women these days seem to feel uncomfortable in relationships of mutual dependence. If you are one of them, I hope you find someone you feel comfortable with. If you wish deeply in your heart, I am sure your wish will be granted.

Others may not like the person you choose to depend on. However, you and that person may be on the same wavelength, and that will make you feel at ease. Such a person may be near you, and may be of the same gender.

Dependence requires getting closer to someone, and this requires courage. I am positive that you can find someone you feel natural and comfortable with to build such a relationship. Once you become comfortable with depending on someone else, you will be able to let others depend on you.

With such great love, which allows others to depend on you, you can expect to become a source for giving hope to people around you.

By looking at the photograph of the water crystal of "hope," you may remember the mother ocean. The memory of the expansive, vast sea may remind you of a state of being surrounded by great love.

When I first saw the picture, I was reminded of my mother's love and of my wife's love, and I felt my love toward them redouble. I felt very much encouraged.

PURPOSE AND DESPAIR

If someone were to ask you, "What do you live for?" how would you respond? Even now I am unable to give an immediate answer. Why? Because the purpose of life changes over time. Try to remember: What did you live for when you were twenty, thirty, or forty? You are very likely to find that it has changed. The life purpose we choose is not necessarily always beautiful and noble.

The water crystal in Figure 2 shows a beautiful hexagon. It indicates the positive nature of what

Figure 2. The outer, feather-like parts have sparkling spots. Is your life purpose something sparkling for you?

makes us feel that life is worth living. What is noticeable in this crystal is that the outer, feather-like parts have sparkling spots. They are unique to this crystal. Perhaps the purpose of life is something that shines on us.

Please take a moment to remember when you found the purpose of your life. When something takes your breath away, when amazement gives you goose bumps, and when an excitement makes you restless, your heart is thrilled. The purpose of life may be found through encountering thrilling experiences; such an encounter is what shines for you.

The purpose of life may further fortify your strengths, or it may complement your weaknesses. If you can develop your strengths more, you will be radiant and feel a greater purpose in life.

As for weaknesses, you might find yourself naturally drawn to something that helps resolve them. As we humans have a sense of balance, we tend to be attracted to what we feel is lacking in ourselves. When you encounter what you were looking for, you will probably find brilliance in it. Thus it will become your life purpose.

An encounter with a person, an encounter with a meaningful job, a dream that you want to chase for the rest of your life—all of these are leading you toward your purpose in life.

On the other hand, when we give up all hope, our immune system weakens, and our natural healing power diminishes.

Initially, I didn't think that water would make a crystal after being shown the word "despair." However, the crystal in Figure 3 looks like the making

Figure 3. This crystal teaches us that any despair has hope within it. It is a sign of hope. In the world of water, there is no such thing as total despair.

of a hexagon. It may be saying that any despair has hope within it. I didn't want to show you the pictures that were too distorted, so I picked a relatively good-looking one.

The water crystal in Figure 3 seems to have shrunk. We, too, shrink when we despair. We stoop down and turn in upon ourselves. However, when we say we despair, feeling despair amounts to perhaps 80 percent, while the remaining 20 percent is our dormant hope.

Though small, a sign of hope does come through in this crystal. In the world of water, I don't believe there is such a thing as total despair because water circulates. Water can pass from one form to another and finally come back to its beauty. So, too, can we humans.

Even when we feel we are at the bottom of despair, we have latent faculties that bounce us back to life and allow us to find the purpose to live again.

THANKS TO (OKAGESAMA)

Strangely, the water crystal in Figure 4 has a shadow. I was surprised because water seemed to capture the word *okagesama* ("thanks to" in Japanese, or more literally "thanks to the shadow of"). Among the water crystal photographs I took, one was shaped like an elephant's trunk and one like the rope ornament of a shrine. I realize that water has a mystical power to show its surroundings.

Figure 4. Okagesama (thanks to the shadow of) is a unique and beautiful Japanese expression of gratitude. As the word indicates, a shadow appeared in this crystal. It's a mysterious phenomenon, isn't it?

Maybe we could say that water is a blueprint of reality. I sincerely think that you can find the systems of the universe in this blueprint.

An important Buddhist text, the Heart Sutra, states, "Form is emptiness; emptiness is form." I take this to mean something that exists is in fact void (emptiness) and void does in fact exist. A shadow is certainly empty. Therefore, I believe that a shadow must have a high potential within itself to create something anew. It is a wonder to me that *okagesama* is an expression used exclusively by the Japanese. It is a beautiful phrase that everybody knows in Japan. The feeling of gratitude contained in *okagesama* gives off positive energy to others and transforms itself into love in their hearts. It would be splendid for people to frequently exchange such a beautiful expression. Have you said *okagesama* lately?

YOU FOOL

"In the beginning was the Word," says the Bible. There is no doubt that words have a strong influence on people. The same is true with water; after being exposed to the words "you fool," water has never formed beautiful crystals.

In the beginning, the world probably had only beautiful and creative words. Thus it must have been filled with creative energies to produce new things. Then the words with negative energies appeared, for example, "you fool" and "no good."

The crystal depicted in Figure 5 gives us the impression of a swirling typhoon with the force to

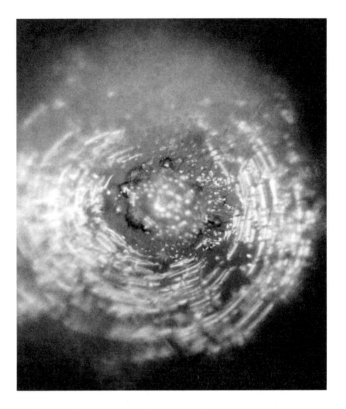

Figure 5. This crystal tells us about the destructive power that negative words carry. Negative words are hurtful not only to humans but also to animals and plants.

destroy everything. Looking at this crystal makes me wonder if saying "you fool" to someone has a similar effect on that person's heart, making it corrupt and ugly like the crystal in this photograph. Simultaneously, the person who calls others names is inevitably tainted by the same negative influence. Words affect our heart and create vibrations. A good vibration creates good energy; a bad vibration amplifies bad energy.

Happiness will never come from a negative and destructive phrase such as this one. Your words have the potential to change everything.

CONFIDENCE

The crystal in Figure 6 makes me realize that confidence is created by the accumulation of experiences. Overconfidence, or behaving with too much confidence not backed up by solid practices, is merely a pretense and bound to be exposed sooner or later. True confidence comes from trusting yourself as well as others. That is how one attains real, unswerving confidence. Having been shown the word "confidence," the water creates a crystal with a complete and beautiful shape. Ideas that have positive energies produce beautiful crystals. We've all heard the saying "Silence is golden." Silence—"no talk but act"—is often valued as a virtue among the Japanese. However, I myself tend

Figure 6. A complete and beautiful crystal resulted from the word "confidence." "Self-trusting," as the word may be defined, has a positive energy.

to "talk and act." I believe that confidence can be built by taking responsible actions after you have announced what you are going to do.

Those who wish to gain confidence may want to look at this water crystal photograph frequently and always have it on hand, perhaps by carrying it in a breast pocket, placing it in a pocketbook, or putting it up on the wall.

．　．　．

True confidence is generated by behaving respon-
sibly. All of your experiences, whether successes or
failures, will turn into confidence that will support
you and help you shine.

I LOVE YOU

The water that was shown the phrase "I love you"
made a big, dynamic crystal, as seen in Figure 7.
This crystal also had a very large, beautiful base.
When a person says to someone, "I love you"—for
example, a mother to her child, a husband to his
wife, or a wife to her husband—the one who hears
the words will shine beautifully. Compared with
crystals that were formed after water was shown the
phrase "love and thanks" (which I'll discuss later),
this one, having been shown "I love you," seems
less restricted. I wonder if it has something to do
with the present progressive form used in Japanese for "I love you": "I *am loving* you."

In love, agape (unconditional, self-sacrificing
love) is often compared with eros (passionate love

Figure 7. This crystal has the expansive feel of growing farther out. By continually being shown "I love you," water yields crystals that grow bigger and shinier.

with sensual desire). I believe that eros is changeable while agape is not. Thus eros can generate more energy. When eros changes into agape, vast love will wrap you in gentle warmth.

Westerners frequently use the expression "I love you," whereas the Japanese don't. Japanese men in middle age or older tend to be especially shy about expressing their love for someone, and may do so only on very rare occasions. I was no exception until about ten years ago, but now I often say it to my employees and family members. Some people say, "Love doesn't have to be expressed in words." For those who have the vibration of divinely pure consciousness, it may be a different story, but most of us ordinary folks are better off verbalizing it.

Of course, the accompanying emotion is important. Water does not respond in beautiful crystals when "I love you" is communicated obligatorily and carelessly. So the best way of saying "I love you" would be to do so naturally and wholeheartedly, when the moment and the emotion arise.

Of course, I hope that women also feel comfortable saying "I love you," without worrying that they are imposing themselves on others. To children, sweethearts, husbands, and friends, women should freely express it. When you say these words, the water inside of you is affected by beautiful radiance.

TOUCHED

The crystal in Figure 8 shows a shape of hands in prayer in one of its outer parts. I believe that people feel touched when their prayers come true, or when their latent desire or hope is fulfilled. I won-

Figure 8. "Touched" implies "feeling grateful and moving." It is a base for a resonance phenomenon. Let's cherish our feeling of being "touched," no matter how small it may be.

der if this is why the shape of prayer appeared in this water crystal. As indicated in the two Japanese characters *(kanji)* that mean "touched"—"feel" and "move"—the word has a strong power to affect our hearts.

Without having experiences of "being touched," people find it difficult to live with vigor and health.

Mrs. Suzue Kato, who lived to be 104 years old, used to say, "Live each and every day having ten 'touched' experiences." Even busy people, I hope, will have at least three "touched" experiences in a day—in the morning, during the day, and in the evening.

One of the most moving experiences I have ever had since I started to take photographs of water crystals was when I saw the picture of a water crystal from Fujiwara Dam. We had initially gone to the dam to collect a sample; the water looked very dirty, as it contained impurities such as bacteria. I couldn't believe my eyes when I saw the picture of an amazingly beautiful crystal. At the time I had no idea why we could take such a beautiful picture. Later it occurred to me that the crystal might have been formed at the level of subatomic particles that we cannot see even with an electron microscope. Yet somehow we were able to capture the picture of it.

Between the soul of the person who took the picture and the intrinsically exquisite energy of the water, there must have been a beautiful phenomenon of resonance. Thus it was possible for us to take the wonderful picture of the water crystal. It was a moving experience for me to understand this. I was also touched by the fact that such a beautiful picture came about due to some power beyond the natural world.

Do you know the character Jean Valjean in *Les Misérables*? He is a criminal who one night steals silver from a church. When the police take him back to the church the next day, the bishop protects Valjean by telling the police that he gave the silver to him and proceeds to hand him some silver candleholders, too. Valjean feels as if he's been struck by lightning. The goodness starts to grow in him. Actually, I would say that what is awakened in him is the innate goodness that has quietly remained within him together with other qualities such as truth and beauty.

As you probably know, after Valjean has this experience, he lives a wonderful life and does many things to help others. I would think that the bishop, who has had such an impact on Valjean, would also receive substantial energy of gratitude in return.

Touching experiences such as these aren't confined to great works of literature, however: they can be found in our daily lives. One example for me was when my company went bankrupt with a 100 million yen—about $1 million—debt. We had a family council that included all of my brothers, and they said, "It will be very difficult to clear such a big debt. You should declare personal bankruptcy and divorce your wife." I felt half-resigned and thought I had no other choice but to accept their advice. In reality, I didn't have the energy to argue. However, my wife decidedly said, "I will not divorce him. I know he can get back on his feet again." For the next seven years, she worked as a saleslady for an insurance company, and we lived off her income. She made it possible for me to focus on working hard to repay my debt.

Perhaps "touching" is an act of love. It is a great gift from the soul for those who live their lives wholeheartedly.

FAMILY LOVE

The crystal in Figure 9 seems to tell us that the ideal family involves three generations—grandparents, parents, and children. I feel that the most beautiful part of this crystal is the faint layer in the background that supports the other two layers. I believe this layer represents grandparents. They are big, but they are not forward. They seem to

Figure 9. This is a unique crystal formed as if showing a family of three generations—grandparents, parents, and children. Family love that gives us strength lasts forever.

shine for their children and grandchildren from the back. What an admirable way of life they are demonstrating!

Modern society seems to give the cold shoulder to grandparents. I don't know how this came about, but it saddens me. This water crystal reminds us of the fact that the parents' and children's generations exist because of grandparents. Although each individual's life is finite, life keeps going forever, from generation to generation in a family. Whether we notice or not, the love of our family, a love that asks nothing in return, is always there to give us great strength.

BENEVOLENCE

Benevolence is a kind of love that symbolizes the affection of parents for their children. The crystal in Figure 10 also shows multiple layers. Behind the one in the foreground, which is growing bigger, there is a larger structure that seems to support the one in front with unstinting love.

Personally, I treasure this word, "benevolence." My father died at the age of fifty-seven, when I was a sophomore in college. He was poor, but he lived frugally to raise his children and send them to college. He was a very loving family man. As far as I know, he had never met his biological parents. He was the illegitimate child of a village headman's daughter in Gigu (which is in the middle of Japan) and a schoolteacher. Soon after his birth, he was abandoned at a brothel. Three months later, the Emoto family adopted him, and

Figure 10. This crystal reminded me of my father. He didn't make himself stand out, but he looked after his children lovingly and with a big heart.

he was raised by loving foster parents. However, his foster mother passed away when he was five years old.

His foster father married another woman, who was also nice, but my father started to feel somewhat uncomfortable after his stepbrothers were born. When he grew up and got a job, he requested a transfer to Tokyo, where he met the woman who was to become my mother.

Until he received the family registration document that he needed in order to marry, my father never knew that he was adopted and that his biological parents were elsewhere. He was shocked and decided to look for his biological mother; after much searching he was able to discover her whereabouts. He visited her husband's family, but he wasn't allowed to meet her. I believe that because he had such a background, he wanted to choose a family-oriented lifestyle. Thanks to my father's choice, my siblings and I grew up very happily, receiving plenty of love from our parents. The inscription on my father's tombstone reads "Lived in benevolence." This is the phrase that we, his children, selected for him. In looking back, I feel his life was a demonstration of this important virtue.

Two

WHO
ARE
YOU?

It has been seventeen years since I first became involved in studying water. During that time—and especially over the past nine years, since I started to take photographs of crystals—water has taught me many things. I learned things about myself, family, work, society, nation, world, universe, energy, life, diseases, the afterlife, and nature. I became quite knowledgeable, and I want to share the important matters I learned from water with as many people as possible.

Thus I walk around the world as if I were a missionary in the Middle Ages or a street preacher in Japan. I wonder if, thanks to modern transportation, I could have done as much work in three years by myself as they did in a hundred years.

Yet I still don't feel that I have walked enough.

I still don't feel that I have talked enough. I wish to continue my journey. However, I have learned from the great Zen priest and poet Ikkyu—his name literally means "a short rest" in Japanese—that it is no good to rush things. I shall take a rest here so that I can organize and write down what I learned from water. I shall pour what is in me onto paper. As I empty my head, I anticipate water's further teachings. I anxiously look forward to my head being filled with delightful knowledge again. With a water refill, I can get back to my enjoyable journey. Till then, please stay with me for a while.

WHO ARE YOU? I AM WATER

Some years back a philosophical novel, *Sophie's World* by Jostein Gaarder, made best-seller lists around the world. In the book there is a question: "Who are you?" Since my childhood, I've asked myself the same question many times. I've wondered who I was and why I was here.

In high school I often discussed these questions (rather naively, I must say) with friends in my literary circle. Our talks would go on late into the night. Alongside these discussions I would read many of the great literary works of Japan and other countries, checking books out of the school library one after another. Among the books I read that had a big impact on me were Fyodor Dostoyevsky's *The Idiot,* Leo Tolstoy's *War and Peace,* and Victor Hugo's *Les Misérables.* But when I went to college, I had different priorities, and I wound up joining the rugby club. Rugby was a lot of fun, and I put all my spare energy into it, so much so that I completely forgot about the questions I had asked earlier in my life. Then I went out into the world.

In the twenty-five years after college, I was an unremarkable workaholic, never resisting or questioning anything about Japan's capitalistic society—the rapid economic growth, the bubble economy that followed, and finally the bursting of the bubble. Eventually, I was beaten and burned out. Though I wasn't conscious of it then, I now see that I had to live an intense life with many ups and downs.

As you might imagine, at this time I was far from asking myself a question such as "Who am I?" My life continued to take twists and turns, but as I worked hard, I was blessed with meeting interesting people.

Eventually, I became independent and started

a small trading company (IHM), which imported medical devices from the United States. It began to change my life completely, and I returned to the frame of mind where I would ask the question "Who am I?"

Now I can clearly answer that question: "I am water." Why and how did I arrive at this answer? I will explain it in the subsequent sections about my work and the events that followed.

WATER AND VIBRATION

I became aware that I am water when my company shifted the products it handled from medical devices to water. For some reason, I was given a great business break dealing with water. I became fascinated by this opportunity, as if I were destined for this work. Because I lacked a background in chemistry and natural science, I began an intense study of water from the perspective of my favorite field, literature.

My inquiry led me to understand that water had a *hado* (vibratory) nature. As a result of this realization, I imported a device for measuring magnetic resonance *(hado)*. I then measured the properties of water using the device, developed a product called *Hado* Water, and established a therapeutic method called *Hado* Water Therapy.

Having achieved remarkable results with *Hado* Water, I wrote a book titled *Hado Jidai eno Jyomaku* (The Prelude to the *Hado* Age) in 1992, six years after my water investigations had commenced.

Although the book was written by an unknown author and published by a small press, it was well received and much talked about, thanks to the introduction and recommendation by Mr. Yukio Funai, chairman of Funai Consulting. It was the first book to introduce the concept of *hado* to the general public.

However, soon after the book was published, disturbing phenomena involving cult groups (including Aum Shinrikyo) became widely discussed in Japan. Some people even started to talk about *hado* in association with them. Moreover, others interpreted *hado* in their own way and introduced many dubious *hado* products to the market.

Like quantum mechanics, *hado* should have been understood as an important science that clarified the root of all phenomena. However, partially due to the efforts of some scientists and authorities, it failed to become accepted in this way.

For that reason I was compelled to find a straightforward way to have the general public understand this essential and fundamental concept. The invisible world of *hado* must be made visible somehow. How could I do it? I contemplated it day after day, even while I was sleeping.

The idea that finally came to me, as you might have guessed, was to freeze water and take pictures of the crystals, as if they were snowflakes.

TAKING PICTURES OF
FROZEN WATER CRYSTALS

It was in July 1994 that the idea hit me. I happened to be reading a Japanese translation of *The Day That Lightning Chased the Housewife: And Other Mysteries of Science* by Julia Leigh and David Savold. At one point they discuss the wonderful fact that no two snowflakes are identical. As I read it, I thought, "I've got it. Snow is water! I must be able to see water crystals if I freeze water."

Immediately, I put the idea into practice at my

company. After two months of struggles, we finally succeeded in taking the first photograph of a water crystal. We went on to perform many experiments, and I indeed learned many things from water. What I learned went into my books, including *Messages from Water, The Hidden Messages in Water, Kessho Monogatari* (Crystal Story), *Mizuwa Kataru* (Water Talk), and *The True Power of Water.*

My hope to see *hado* take root has progressed just to the first stage, but it was realized nonetheless. *Hado* has become a term that many readers of my books understand and use. This work has also taught me even more important things, some of which cause a sort of cultural shock to many people when I share them.

THE RATIO OF WATER
IN A HUMAN BODY

Let's get into the core subject: Why are we water? As you know, 70 percent of the human body is water. Of course, the percentage differs depending on age; the younger the person is, the higher the percentage. For example, a newborn baby's body is more than 80 percent water. When a human life begins as a fertilized egg, the percentage of water is about 96 percent. On average, the percentage of water in an adult's body is 70 percent. It goes down to about 60 percent when a person reaches sixty years of age. As we grow older, the percentage of water in our bodies is further reduced, and the skin wrinkles more. In Japanese, a person with young and fresh skin is described as *mizumizushii hito* (a person full of water). (Incidentally, the next-highest atom is carbon, which counts for 10 percent, followed by nitrogen at 2.4 percent.)

When the amount of water in the body drops below 50 percent, the physical body ends its life. My mother had a long life and lived to be ninety-three years old. In the last five years of her life, her body became smaller and smaller. Shrinking must have been her genes' strategy to keep her body's water level above the required 50 percent. By understanding the relationship between age and the amount of water in the body, one can see why water is considered the source of life.

Because water is the single largest component in human beings, we can say we are water. Please remember this point, as it will be the premise for understanding the rest of this book.

Let me repeat: "We are made up of water."

Three

THE
BEGINNING
OF
LOVE

THE ESSENTIALS FOR
ALL BEINGS

The earth's environment is filled with wonders. Why are we always surrounded by oxygen, water, and moderate temperatures? How does our planet constantly move in an orbit? It is indeed amazing.

What's more, a vast number of beings exist on earth. There are more than six billion people; domesticated animals such as dogs, cats, cattle, horses, sheep, pigs, and chickens; wild animals such as monkeys, raccoons, foxes, deer, bears, lions, tigers, panthers, giraffes, elephants, camels, kangaroos, and snakes; birds such as sparrows, peacocks, hawks, and butcher-birds; and insects such as ladybugs and other beetles. Additionally, there are reptiles, small creatures like earthworms and microbes, fish, sea creatures, plants, and minerals.

There are so many beings on this earth that it's impossible to list them all. Why are there so many? How were they born? Why do they exist? Only God knows the answers to these questions. Yet even though there are so many beings, they all have one thing in common. Every one of them has energy. From another point of view, we could say, "Everything is made by energy." In other words, all beings need energy. What, then, is that energy?

WHAT WAS THE BEGINNING OF ALL?

Let me tell you the conclusion first: energy means vibration. All beings are made up of atoms, and all atoms vibrate at their core. Each and every thing is vibrating. Yes, I mean everything—a dog, a cat, and a computer. Also, I mean a book, a plant, clothes, shoes, and perfume, as well as bread, rice, and everyday dishes.

Things exist because of vibration. Therefore, vibration is energy. An atom, a vibrating atom, invariably makes a sound. A pebble at the roadside, too, is vibrating and making a sound. A beautiful tulip blooming in your garden is also making a sound. For that matter, even the book you are now holding is making a sound. Still, we cannot hear these sounds, because we are not designed to hear them.

The Divine that created human beings designed our hearing abilities within the range of 15 hertz (fifteen vibrations per second) to 20,000 hertz. This is called the range of audible sounds. The Creator must have made this arrangement so that we could sleep at night. What if we could hear the sounds that a bed or a pillow gives off constantly? Surely, we would have difficulty sleeping.

Another important point is that vibration means life. The Japanese character (*kanji*) for "life" has the symbol meaning "to beat" at its center. This character must have been developed to show that beating is necessary to continue life, because vibration means life. In another sense, life also means rhythm.

How are we informed of someone's death? A doctor takes the person's pulse and says, "I am sorry, but he is dead." Death is pronounced when the heart stops beating.

The issue of brain death is controversial. I do not believe that brain death is really death, nor do I think that someone in the vegetable state is dead. When the heart's beating or vibration stops, that is death. Unless the heart stops beating, or vibrating, a doctor cannot pronounce death.

From this point of view, we can say, "Everything in this world is alive." We tend to think that only the things that move and grow are living. If we take the view that vibration equals life, even a pebble at the roadside is decisively alive. Perhaps Kannon (the goddess of mercy in Buddhism) sees the world that way. Literally speaking, the name Kannon means "one who can observe all sounds"—not hear them, only observe or see all sounds. Thus, I suppose, she teaches that "all things have life; so love and respect them."

Then where does vibration come from? The Japanese character for "sound" has two parts: "to stand" and "the sun." The character points out that the source of energy is the sun. Not until the sun "stands" does a sound, or vibration, exist. The sun is the source of all energies. No wonder so many parts of the world have the practice of worshipping the sun, including Amaterasu Omikami (goddess of the sun) in Japan.

THE SECRETS OF VIBRATION
(SOUND)

Since 1987, when I started to import magnetic resonance analyzers (MRAs), I have been a *hado* and water researcher. For the next ten years I devoted all my energies to making *hado* water and helping more than fifteen thousand people recover from illness.

When I published *Messages from Water* (which included the world's first water crystal photograph) in June 1999, I became more confident about my concept of *hado,* having seen many people appreciate what I had to offer in that book. Today many sad and confusing things are happening in the world. Thinking about what is going to happen next gives me some anxiety and fear. However, I believe that we can deepen our understanding of the world by simply understanding the nature of vibration (sound). Vibration has many secrets, and once we understand its nature, we will understand many things about life and human beings. My theory of vibration consists of three parts: resonance, purity, and similarity. The various phenomena in the world, I believe, can be understood by using

Figure 11. Tuning fork.

these three concepts. Allow me to explain them one by one.

GETTING ENERGIZED— RESONANCE

In musical terms, tuning means to put instruments into proper pitch, as needs to be done in an orchestra. A tuning fork is a device used for this purpose. The device has the shape shown in Figure II.

A tuning fork is made to give off a fixed tone when struck. The most commonly used tuning

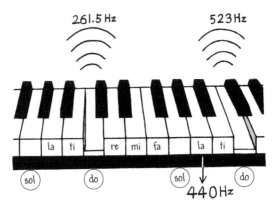

Figure 12. Top: Resonate. Middle: Hit (below 261.5 hertz and 523 hertz). Bottom left to right on the keys: la, ti, re, mi, fa, la, ti. Bottom left to right below the keys: sol, do, sol, do.

fork is one of 440 hertz. (Lately, 442 hertz is a more common frequency for tuning. Due to the change in the earth's terrestrial magnetism, the tone our ears can hear most easily seems to be rising.)

As shown in Figure 12, 440 hertz is the sound of the first A note on a piano keyboard above middle C. The sound of 261.5 hertz is the middle C, and its multiple of two, 523 hertz, is the C one octave above. As for A, it goes from a low pitch of 27.5 hertz to higher pitches of 55, 110, 220, 440, 880, 1,760, 3,520 hertz, and so on.

Let's suppose we have two tuning forks of 440

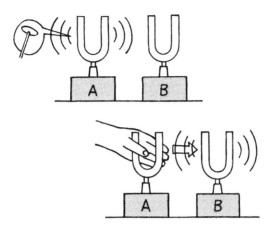

Figure 13. Top: Hit. Energy = vibration. Bottom: Energy from A to B. B continues to vibrate even after A is
stopped.

hertz (Figure 13). When a tuning fork of 440 hertz
is hit with a rubber hammer, we will hear the note
A. When the fork is grabbed to stop the sound, the
other tuning fork of 440 hertz, which is near the
first one, will start to make the sound even though
it is not hit. When both tuning forks have the same
frequency, the second one invariably echoes auto-
matically. This phenomenon is called resonance.

It is an awesome phenomenon, if you think
about it. The second tuning fork is neither hit nor
touched, but it starts to vibrate, even though it is
made out of hard steel that has a large mass. This
phenomenon is proof that energy is vibration.

In 2003, the Nobel Prize in Medicine was given to the two scholars who developed magnetic resonance imaging (MRI). Resonance is used in MRI. It is also a basic principle of physics and has a broad potential for technological application, such as in the development of a device for finding a school of fish in the sea.

ENERGY EXCHANGE—PURITY

Now let's switch one of the two tuning forks to 442 hertz and do the same thing as we did above. The tuning fork of 440 hertz is hit with a rubber hammer. This time, the second one does not seem to give off a sound. However, if we listen very carefully, we can hear a faint vibration. Though the sound is difficult to hear, the second tuning fork is resonating with the first one.

To our ears, the tone of 440 hertz sounds the same as that of 442 hertz. The difference is only 2 hertz, yet it makes a big difference in terms of resonance. In other words, the amount of energy produced drops significantly, and productivity goes down.

If we were to change the tuning fork of 442

hertz to 445 hertz and repeat the process, there would be no resonance. We would not be able to hear even a faint sound. When two things have exactly the same frequency, their resonance is perfect. They can enhance each other's energy in a pure manner.

If their frequency is absolutely the same, two items can attract and communicate with each other; distance is almost irrelevant. This phenomenon is called energy exchange. For example, some mobile phones can be used to call overseas, while others can't. The difference is due to the purity of the frequency transmitted by the phone.

The same is true with people's thoughts. When we tune in to the same thoughts or prayers together, we can expect to generate powerful energy. The world population is approximately 6 billion. How powerful can it be if 10 percent, or 600 million people, hope and pray for something wonderful?

VIBRATION (SOUND)—SIMILARITY

All things are vibrating; thus they have sounds. This means we can sort everything on a scale according to its sound. The scale I mean is the musical scale of "do, re, mi, fa, sol, la, ti, do." On the keyboard of a piano, the black keys are halftones raised from do, re, fa, sol, and la in the key of C major. When halftones are included, we have twelve basic notes within an octave.

This means that we can recognize only twelve different kinds of sounds with our ears. Interestingly, there are twelve signs of the zodiac and twelve horary signs in Chinese astrology.

. . .

Let's take two tuning forks—in this case, one of 523 hertz (a higher "do" of C major) and the other of 261.5 hertz (a lower "do" of C major). When we hit the tuning fork of 523 hertz with a rubber hammer, the tuning fork of 261.5 hertz will resonate. The reverse is also true.

What does this mean? The tuning forks of two different frequencies resonate. A note of "do" on a musical scale resonates with any other "do." No matter how high or low the other "do" may be, as long as it is "do," it resonates. Notes that have the relationship of octave intervals resonate with each other. What does the relationship of octave intervals mean? It's the relationship of notes in which each successive note has a frequency of vibration twice that of the previous, lower note.

For example, the notes that have the relationship of octave intervals of 100 hertz are 200, 400, 800, 1,600, 3,200, 6,400, 12,800, 25,600, 51,200, 102,400, 204,800, 409,600, 819,200 hertz, and so on. The numbers go on from the original number to ones multiplied by 2, 4, 8, 16, and so on.

I call this relationship "the similarity in vibration."

The important point here is that everything has a sound; therefore, we can say every phenomenon and every object has a relationship of similarity with something else. A simple example can be found in the relationship of a violin, a viola, a cello, and a contrabass.

In an atom, electrons circulate around the core. In the solar system, the planets circulate around the sun. These are other examples of the similarity relationship.

WHAT IS OUR SOURCE?

The existence of subatomic particles has been well known for some time. Dr. Masatoshi Koshiba, a Nobel Prize winner in 2002, and others have contributed to this knowledge. The size of a particle is as minute as $^1/_{100,000,000}$ of an atom, which is 0.1 nanometer (10^{-9} m). Naturally, the world of subatomic particles is invisible and inaudible to us. It is a world that most of us have difficulty understanding or even imagining.

Let's think about it, however. Does every phenomenon start big or small? Of course, the answer is the latter. In the case of us humans, our birth may be said to begin with a fertilized egg, when a mother's egg meets with a father's sperm. Do you know the size of the egg? It is currently thought to be 0.1 mm to 0.2 mm, a size that we can barely see with our naked eyes.

However, I believe that our start can actually be found at a much smaller state. That's right, we begin at the size of a subatomic particle. Everything begins at the subatomic particle level, the smallest unit recognized today. It is often said that we should go back to our origins when we get lost. It seems that today we are lost as a natural consequence of a materialistic development process. Now may be the time for us to go back to our origin as subatomic particles and reconsider which is the right path to take.

Some people may argue, "It certainly sounds all right in theory. But how much do we know about subatomic particles anyway? We hardly know them. How is it possible to think about the un-known world?"

The science of such a field is quantum me-chanics. Roughly speaking, the conclusion that this science has arrived at so far is: "The world of quanta (subatomic particles) is chaotic, because the observation results vary depending on the ob-servers."

I think of it differently. My idea is the concept of similarity that we have been discussing in this section. More specifically, it is the similarity of vi-bration. This concept leads to the idea of the hu-man body as a microcosm.

I saw a wonderful videotape that led me to this idea. It was called *Powers of Ten* and produced for IBM more than twenty-five years ago. Easy-to-understand computer graphics presented visually the relationship of similarity between a human body and the cosmos. I believe you can now find

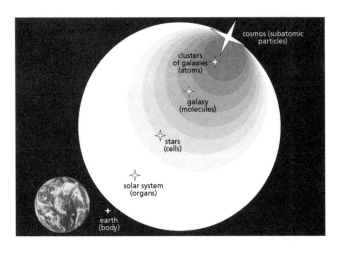

Figure 14.

this film on the Internet, and I highly recommend that you watch it.

Based on my memory of the film, I had a colleague at my company's laboratory make the drawing shown in Figure 14. Only recently have we begun to understand the size of subatomic particles. It is therefore amazing that the film had its origins fifty years ago in a 1957 essay by Kees Boeke.

As discussed earlier, everything, be it a particle or an atom, is vibrating and making a sound, and all sounds are included in the scale of "do" to "do." I have no hesitation in saying this, because there is no sound that is not included in the scale of do, re, mi, fa, sol, la, ti, do. (Of course, there are in-between sounds, such as halftones between "do" and "re," but even these sounds are included in the scale.) Even the sounds in the world of subatomic particles are expressed along the scale of do, re, mi, fa, sol, la, ti, do.

When we accept the human body is a microcosm, we can no longer say that we don't understand the world of subatomic particles. If we view the human body in smaller and smaller increments, we can see that it goes from cell to molecule to atom and finally to subatomic particle. The smallest unit of consciousness and material is a subatomic particle.

Subatomic particles are influenced by our consciousness (positive thoughts, love, and gratitude), good water, and good music. If we shift our path toward deepening our understanding of the science of vibration, we may be able to go back to our origin.

LOVE MEANS GIVING A VIBRATION

Many people became interested in the method of showing words to water and taking pictures of frozen water crystals after reading *Messages from Water*. Naturally, while many people accepted this unconventional method, many others were skeptical. What I most wanted to present in the book was the fundamental meaning of vibration. In *The Hidden Messages in Water* I wrote:

> All things vibrate, and they vibrate at their own frequencies. When you understand this, you will significantly broaden your understanding of the universe . . . In the scientific world of quantum mechanics, it is common knowledge that substances are basically nothing more than vibration. When we look at a substance in an increasingly microscopic manner, we reach the mysterious world where everything is both particles and waves.
>
> Suppose you have a microscopic body and you are off to explore how the universe is made. When you are reduced to the size of an atom, you will only see that electrons are revolving around atomic nuclei. An atom has its own unique frequency according to the number and configuration of electrons. Whatever it is, in the microscopic

world, you will feel everything is not solid, but moving waves. Everything is constantly vibrating and blinking at super high speed.

In the same book, I commented on the relationship between vibration and photographs of water crystals:

> How should we explain that water changes its crystals after being exposed to the words written on paper? A written word itself has its own vibration, and water is sensitive to that vibration. Water can accurately copy the vibration of all things in this world and make invisible vibrations visible to our eyes. When water is shown a word written on paper, it catches the word's vibration and expresses the image in a specific shape.

Among the words that water was exposed to, "love and thanks" sparked the most beautiful response. In *The Hidden Messages in Water*, I explained it as follows:

> The most beautiful crystal we have ever obtained was from the water shown the words

"Love & Thanks." Of course, "Love" alone results in a beautiful crystal. However, when both "Love & Thanks" together are shown, the water crystal added grace to beauty. As if it were a diamond, the crystal sparkled radiantly. Relatively speaking, the water crystal of "Love & Thanks" looked more like the crystal of "Gratitude" than that of "Love." It means that the water crystal reflected a more powerful and stronger influence of "Thanks" it received.

Love is a more active energy. Love is an act of giving heartfelt, unconditional affection. On the other hand, gratitude is a more passive energy—being thankful for something, or thankful for being allowed to live. In one of his poems, Housai Ozaki says, "No container I have, / With my hands I receive." As depicted in his poem, gratitude, I believe, is an act of receiving securely with both hands.

Love and thanks have the relationship of yin and yang. If love is the sun, gratitude is the moon. If love is male, gratitude is female.

WHAT IS OUR ROLE?

The topic of love and gratitude is my favorite, and I always include it in my talks. In general, people express feelings of wonder and acceptance. Lately, I have talked about it along the following lines: Love touches the other person's heart, and the other person responds in gratitude. Like an echo, these feelings move back and forth between people. In nature and the universe, this complementary relationship seems to exist. It is based on the phenomena I observed in my tuning-fork experiments.

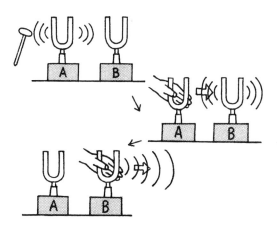

Figure 15. Top: Hit. Middle: Stop. Bottom: Echo phenomenon.

As shown in Figure 15, after tuning fork A of 440 hertz is hit with a rubber hammer, it is grabbed to stop its vibration. Then tuning fork B starts to vibrate. Tuning fork A transmitted the energy to tuning fork B.

Next, tuning fork B is grabbed to stop its vibration. Tuning fork A, which had stopped vibrating, now vibrates. This is the echo phenomenon. One tuning fork is hit, and then the other one vibrates and gives off a sound. The energy of vibration generated by A causes B to vibrate. Isn't the resonance between these two objects like a love-and-gratitude relationship?

Love is in all acts of cheering up others or giving them energy. Therefore, our role is to give energy to others. In other words, our role is to love everything. By doing so, we try to coordinate all things to be in harmony. I believe this is the way to live and this is the divine role we have been given to play on this globe. By making the most beautiful crystal when shown "love and thanks," water renders this concept visible.

All things, including human beings, are incapable of vibrating on their own, so let's give love to others unsparingly.

Four

THE
JOURNEY
OF
WATER

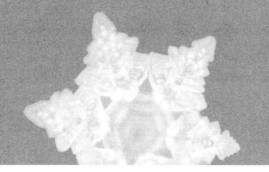

WONDERS OF WATER

No matter how small and powerless we may feel, as long as the energy we give off is pure and continuous, I believe we can change the whole universe at any given phase according to our will.

Why can water catch the vibration we give off in such a pure manner? Have you ever thought about what water is? Perhaps many would say, "No, I haven't, because water is water. It is such a common commodity." That's true. I myself had never thought about water until I became involved with it professionally. As you learn more about water, you will discover what a wondrous commodity it is. Suppose there is a glass of water in front of you. You put an ice cube in the water. The ice floats, doesn't it? Like many others, you may not think much of it. However, it is truly wondrous.

Normally, the density of substances is higher—that is, heavier—in the solid state than in the liquid state. Therefore, with most substances, the solid doesn't float, but sinks in the liquid. Water, however, is different. Specifically, the density of water is said to be 1 g/cm^2, whereas that of ice is 0.92 g/cm^2.

Moreover, in general the density of a substance decreases as the temperature increases. The density of water, however, is highest—in other words, heaviest—at the temperature of $4°$C.

Specific heat is the amount of heat required to raise the temperature of 1 g of a substance by $1°$C. This is also more familiarly known as a calorie. The specific heat of water is the highest among substances. Also, the surface tension of water is so strong that it produces a capillary phenomenon. Among its many wondrous properties, water is an excellent solvent. Water can dissolve and carry most everything; there is no other substance that can do this.

While these properties are understood scientifically, the fundamental reasons for these behaviors have yet to be discovered. The one thing we know is that these properties are very important to support life.

If ice were heavier than liquid water, it would cover the bottoms of the lakes and the seas in the polar regions. If seas and lakes were to freeze from the bottom upward, they would form a gigantic mass of ice, which would not allow the creation of life.

However, because water is heaviest at 4°C, the bottoms of the lakes and seas are maintained at 4°C even in the coldest weather. In terms of specific heat, water ranks the highest among substances. Water's boiling point of 100°C means that it is not easily vaporized. Because of this property, water shortage does not happen rapidly, and a sudden increase is prevented in body and earth temperatures. Water works wonderfully well in retaining heat (when a substance vaporizes, it requires heat).

Moreover, the surface tension of water is so strong that it produces capillary action. This means that water can go up to the tops of tall trees against the force of gravity. This property of water is indispensable to maintaining life. A good example of water's great dissolving ability is the blood in our bodies. Because of water, in the form of blood, necessary nutrients (vibrations needed for each cell) can be distributed all over the body.

Indeed, water has many wondrous properties. Most of these properties are needed for the formation and maintenance of life. As I mentioned earlier, we still don't know why water has such properties. This reality seems to be reflected in the fact that this field has never produced a Nobel Prize winner.

We are water—and yet we hardly understand it. As a result, we don't know ourselves very well, either.

Maybe this is why, after tens of thousands of years of human history, we still engage in acts of war and killing which are against divine Providence. We need to understand water.

Other fields of science have made great progress. Now we need to collect all human intelligence to understand water, the source of life and the "one basic stuff for everything in nature," as the Greek philosopher Thales said. When our questions are answered, we will be able to understand ourselves. The first step is to know the origin of water.

. . .

My book *Hado no Shinri* (The Truth of *Hado*), published in 1994, is not yet available in English and so would not be familiar to readers of my other titles. Since the concepts presented in that book are the foundation for my current thinking, let me cite some relevant passages.

HOW LONG HAS WATER BEEN ON THE EARTH?

I have come to realize that we know almost nothing about water, the source of all life-forms on this planet. I have set forth the theory "water equals *hado*"; therefore, if we don't understand water, we don't understand *hado*, either.

Essentially, I thought that the mystery of water had been solved a long time ago. While I was contemplating deeply why water was so different from other substances and why it had such a complex and incomprehensible nature, I got an inspiration. It occurred to me that maybe the water on this earth came from another planet in the universe!

Later, I found the answer had already been

given by Dr. Louis A. Frank of the University of Iowa in his book *The Big Splash*. As a matter of fact, one of my staff members had given me a copy of the book a few months before I had my inspiration, saying, "This is a very interesting book. I hope you will read it." It ended up on my bookshelf.

The following is a brief biography of Dr. Frank.

Louis A. Frank was born in Chicago in 1938 and became professor of physics at the University of Iowa. Since his involvement in the calibration of the first U.S. lunar probe, he has been an experimenter or investigator for instruments on more than forty spacecraft. The types of instruments include those for energetic charged particles, plasmas, and auroral imaging, which led him to his recent discovery of comets.

Dr. Frank's accomplishments have put him on the cutting edge of plasma research and include the first direct measurements of the terrestrial ring current and of the polar cusp, the current systems in earth's magnetotail, the plasma tori at Jupiter and at Saturn, and global imaging of earth's auroral zones and atmosphere.

Dr. Frank was the first to observe with a scientific instrument the belt of ions around the earth that is now known as the ring current. And he discovered the theta aurora.

Currently, Dr. Frank serves on various NASA space programs and is a member of the National Academy of Sciences, the American Physical Society, the American Astronomical Society, and the American Association for the Advancement of Science.

Dr. Frank is an active scientist and has many brilliant achievements. This well-known scientist, who used to hold conservative opinions, published his findings in *The Big Splash.* The promotional copy on the book cover of the Japanese version reads as follows: "Humans were born from the storms of small comets poured on earth."

Every minute, twenty small comets of about a hundred tons come into the earth's atmosphere. The comets that arrived on the earth over four billion years ago created the rivers, lakes, and oceans. The necessary materials for life were also brought by these comets. A temporary increase in the number of comets contributed to the Ice Age, when dinosaurs and other creatures died out. It's a long-awaited book by a world-renown physicist, in

which his new theory explodes the common knowledge on the origin of the earth.

.   .   .

Dr. Frank's new theory flatly denied the belief that
water was on the earth all along. If it is correct, it
will shake up today's physical chemistry, and it will
inevitably lead to *hado* science.

At the time *Hado no Shinri* (The Truth of *Hado*)
was published, Dr. Frank's theory (expressed in *The
Big Splash*) was considered to be merely his personal
opinion, and his book was published in the private
sector, not within the scientific community. However, NASA officially announced this theory in
May 1997. It was picked up by major news agencies
such as the Associated Press and distributed widely
throughout the world. In Japan, the news was
broadcast by NHK (Japan Broadcasting Corpo-
ration) and was picked up by many national and
local newspapers.

.   .   .

The following is an excerpt from an article that appeared in the evening edition of the *Asahi Shimbun*
newspaper on June 2, 1997:

NASA Observed and Announced: Snowballs from the Universe, Supplies for Seawater?

On May 28, the National Aeronautics and Space Administration (NASA) announced that its polar satellite took pictures of numerous small astronomical bodies like snowballs falling into the atmosphere of the earth. These snowballs are small astronomical bodies with a diameter of around fifteen meters. Every day, thousands of them fly in and become parts of clouds as they get closer to the earth's surface. Considering the length of time since the birth of the earth, these astronomical bodies were possibly the source of seawater . . .

In 1986, Dr. Louis Frank of the University of Iowa claimed that water originated from the universe based on photographs taken by a U.S. satellite. His view was not widely accepted, due to lack of evidence.

Three months later, the Institute for Astronomy at the University of Hawaii made an announcement endorsing Dr. Frank's theory. On August 24, 1997, the morning edition of the *Mainichi Shimbun* newspaper reported as follows:

Comets Are the Mother of the Sea

The Institute for Astronomy at the University of Hawaii stated that their observation of the Hyakutake and Hale-Bopp comets yielded results in support of the theory that "the comets fallen to the earth are the source of seawater." The announcement was made at the General Assembly of the International Astronomical Union held in Kyoto on the twenty-third . . .

Mr. Junichi Watanabe, Section Chief, Public Information Office, National Astronomical Observatory of Japan, said, "It is very convincing that two comets yielded similar results. While all seawater may not be from comets, it can be said that comets played an important role in the formation of the sea."

SO WE ARE ALIENS

If water is, in fact, not a material intrinsic to earth, our biological origin and evolution must be explained quite differently from the way they are explained today. One thing regarded as absolutely true in today's science is that "no life can be born or maintained without water." I believe this is 100 percent correct, and no one would argue about it. If so, it can be said that all life-forms, including humans, have their origin outside of the earth.

Once this new theory of water origin is accepted, many fields—such as biology, anthropology, physics, astronomy, medicine, psychology, theology, chemistry, and pedagogy—will have to completely revise their textbooks. It will be too much to take for scientists who believe that water originated on earth, because it will undermine many of their accomplishments. Ignoring the new theory might be an easy solution. Despite the reports made by two authoritative sources, NASA and the University of Hawaii, no one seems to have dealt squarely with it.

However, by accepting the new theory, we have a chance to understand many inexplicable mysteries in our history. For example, there are the stories that continents such as Atlantis, Lemuria, and Mu existed but were lost underwater. Many undersea ruins were discovered in the Sakishima Islands of Japan. Could they be the proofs of such stories? How authentic is the allegedly true history in the old Takeuchi documents and Heitate shrine of Mount Aso in Japan? How about a new theory regarding when the pyramids and the sphinxes were built? What is the true nature of the photon belt? If a catastrophe will come, when will it take place? These questions may be answered if we assume that human beings originated outside of the earth. By understanding this correctly, our alternatives will be expanded because our view of human history will shift from the earth to the universe.

I feel I have a role to play in this shift, because it will be difficult for scientists to take up such daring ideas within the framework of today's society. I am free; I have no constraints to worry about and no honor to be damaged. Even if others think I am crazy, I don't care. I just do not want to live my life without expressing what I think.

Even if my theory should turn out to be off the mark, it will not hurt anyone, as it has a positive nature. In such a case, I imagine that the Divine would scold and forgive me, simply saying, "You careless man."

OUR TRUE HOME—
THE BIG DIPPER

Let's start a fairy tale with the assumption that water came from the universe to the earth and resulted in the birth of human beings.

How did we come to this planet? I believe we came to earth on comets, as in the NASA report. Well, "on comets" may not be accurate. Perhaps I should say "in the form of water crystals in comets." A water crystal is like a phantom because it disappears at 0°C. With a microscope, we can see water crystals at temperatures between -15°C and 1°C. The shape of crystals is three-dimensional. I wonder if frozen water crystals are between three- and four-dimensional.

Water in liquid form is like a state where we humans are living, and water in crystal form is a state where we are spirit. Perhaps when water is transmitted, it is in a four-dimensional state. Somewhere in the universe, water is sent in the form of ice in a four-dimensional state. As it gets closer to the earth, the temperature increases, and it assumes a three-and-a-half-dimensional state. When it arrives, it becomes liquid in a three-dimensional state.

As you know, water changes its form within the atmosphere on earth. These forms include haze, fog, hail, snow, cloud, sleet, ice, and liquid water. I think the changes that water goes through in the universe are far more numerous than we can imagine. In this vein, I even wonder if light could be a form of water.

The question is where in the universe we came from and why. I originally thought that we were exiles of the universe because we seem to have a hard time giving up our egos and sins. Let me cite the following, again from *Hado no Shinri* (The Truth of Hado).

ARE WE THE DESCENDANTS OF EXILES OF THE UNIVERSE?

Could we be the descendants of exiles of the universe? Could it be possible that our ancestors committed a crime on a faraway star in the universe?

Perhaps that star was like a utopia. Our ancestors, however, happened to develop ego, and committed a crime. According to the rule there, they were banished. Their destination was determined by the degree of their crime. Of course, there is no way of knowing where earth ranked. However, earth might have been for major criminals, because under the spell of gravity on earth it is impossible to escape.

Our ancestors were changed into ice and blasted off to earth. After an unimaginably long trip, they finally came close to earth like a comet and flew into the atmosphere. Naturally, the heat melted our ancestors in the form of ice, and they vaporized instantaneously. Then they became clouds and eventually arrived as rain on the earth's surface for the first time. After an unimaginably long time, they were born as human beings. As they lost all memories of the past, they had to start their lives all over again and build civilization.

Under the influence of gravity, which might have contributed to the formation of the yin and yang theory, we cannot get off earth so easily, and we are currently at the crucial moment. This story ends here.

Lately, however, I have developed a theory that

we are graduates from the school of the universe.
I have grown uncomfortable with the earlier story
that we are the descendants of exiles because of its
negativity.

ARE WE GRADUATES FROM THE
SCHOOL OF THE UNIVERSE?

What if we were sent to earth as missionaries, not
as the descendants of exiles? Let me introduce another story, using myself as an example:

I was born on a star far, far away from the
earth. The star was much more peaceful and advanced than the earth. The star had a missionary
system, and everyone had to teach its precepts on
the other stars or planets.

When I graduated from school, I perhaps
wrote a thesis that said, "My mission is to go to
earth to spread love." I received a passing grade
and graduated from the school of the universe. A
planetary rocket was launched to Japan, since I requested Japan to be my destination. As usual, all
of my memories were erased, except for the necessary information to become a human, which was
left in the crystals of ice. In terms of geophysics,

the distance between my home star and earth was enormous. Perhaps, due to a different dimension of time, I arrived at earth instantaneously.

On July 22, 1943, I made my first cry as a child of my parents, Hiroshi and Kazu Emoto. (The first cry of a newborn baby is 440 hertz—I remember having read it in a book. This cry may be a signal to let the home star know of a baby's safe arrival.)

I grew up in a loving environment, receiving my parents' deep love and understanding. The most important period is believed to be the first ten years of life, when cranial nerves fully develop and stabilize in a human. I was blessed with having good brothers, and my childhood was filled with the pleasures of a happy home, even though we were poor.

I was the youngest of my parents' four children. My parents, my father in particular, tended to be stricter with my brothers, but I was raised freely and easily. I am really grateful for the way my parents brought me up.

In my youth, I was a serious student who also very much enjoyed music and sports. I liked to play musical instruments, and I was clever with my hands, which made me a quick learner. This experience seems to have helped me later in my work with MRA, the *hado*-measuring device, which was like a musical instrument.

After I went into the world, I worked very hard. My hard work resulted in both successes and failures. For the first twenty-five years, I experienced many ups and downs. I made my wife, who is my business partner as well, go through hardships, including a bankruptcy with a large debt and so many other difficulties that I cannot list them all here. She cheered me up by saying that these are the results of trying to be "right and just."

In retrospect, I now realize that these hardships were touchstones leading me to my current work. During those twenty-plus years, I stood at the crossroads many times. When I had to decide to go right or left, I made my choices based on what was "right and just." As if it were a game, I chose right or left at each intersection and came to the place where MRA and *hado* technology were.

After all, I hadn't forgotten my thesis upon graduating from the school of the universe. My work has just begun, but I feel that I have reached the door of the house of my destination. I knocked at the door, and the door opened smoothly. I feel I am in the first room.

I have no idea how many more rooms there are, but I feel excited, like the leader of an expedition team. My intention is to go as far as I can and to broadcast what I see to as many people as possible.

I keenly think about the importance of childhood upbringing. I owe the role I am playing now to my parents' unconditional love.

CHILDREN, THE GIFT
FROM THE DIVINE

Let's continue the story of the graduates from the school of the universe. Since I was born on July 22, 1943, I must have arrived on earth during the fall equinox of 1942. So I graduated from the school of the universe about sixty-five years ago. My home star must also be constantly advancing. Therefore, even if the information I brought with me from the star were fully revealed, it is already sixty-five years old. (If I had an excellent antenna to receive up-to-date correspondence courses from my home star, it would be a different story, but I don't think I do.)

Let's think about the babies arriving today.

They graduated from the school of the universe some sixty years later than I did. They are awesome, because they exist on this planet with information potentially more advanced than we currently have.

What should those of us who came here earlier do for the newly arrived babies? They must also have written their theses. Therefore, we need to secure the environment so that the newly arrived will not forget their missions. Let's put our hopes in them. Let's trust them. Let's not force wrong education on them. Let's provide them with a comfortable and healthy environment. It is our role to prepare such a field for them. What specifically should we do? The following is my ten-point proposal for future education:

1. Let's remember that adults do not own a child, just because he or she is temporarily entrusted to them by the Divine.

2. Let's not compare our children with other children and worry about the differences.

3. Each child has written his or her own thesis. Each thesis is different and reflects its writer's personality. The role of an adult as a guardian

is to fully bring out the child's unique individuality.

4. The first ten years of the child's life are especially important, because cranial nerve cells keep developing during that time. By observing attentively, you will understand what the child wants or what his or her actions are for. Let's try to understand the child as much as possible. If we can't, let's not worry by ourselves. Let's find a support group and learn together.

5. Let's select our children's kindergarten and elementary school from the children's viewpoint, not from the parents'. When children are three or four years old, they can express their own opinions. The role of adults is to provide children with the correct information and alternatives, and let them make their decision.

6. Let's refrain from using negative expressions such as "don't" and "no good." Instead, let's use more positive expressions such as "let's" and "shall we." If we understand the princi-

ples of *hado,* we will know how much influence our words have on our children's positive thinking.

7. Let's treat a child not as a child but as a person with a sound personality, including consciousness and responsibilities.

8. Let's think together with a child when he or she asks "why?" Perhaps we won't be able to answer many of the questions, but it would be wonderful to make it a habit to learn and think with the child. Let's not make irresponsible remarks. Especially in the realm of natural sciences, let's study until we can answer the child's questions confidently.

9. Let's pay attention to the information coming by electromagnetic waves. But keep in mind that when the information is bad, children may receive fatally bad influences. Let's give children no violent TV programs and games.

10. It is important for adults to have their own clear understanding of sexuality (though it may be difficult to do so). If necessary, let's share our understanding with children with-

out flinching. The children's resolute attitude, more than what the parents say, will give
them a good signpost.

ALL LIVES ALSO CAME
FROM THE UNIVERSE

Water didn't exist on the earth in the beginning. If
water is the source of everything, as Thales, a
Greek philosopher, said, not only human beings
but all other lives that require water have their origin somewhere in the universe. Of course, I have
no way of knowing if it was the Divine who sent us
to the earth. We weren't just sent to the desolate
wild earth without water. Whoever it was had a kind
heart to program the basic necessities in water so
that we could live on this planet. Dogs may hold
the key to evidence of some sort of divine inter-
vention.

For example, unlike for many other animals,
the Japanese character (kanji) for "dog" doesn't
have a part indicating animals. According to a story
I heard directly from Dr. Hoang Van Duke, a
medical scientist originally from Vietnam and a

professor emeritus at the University of Southern California, what is implied in the Japanese character for "dog" is that Heaven (God) sent dogs to earth to have them help human beings and let them be good cooperators. As dogs are sent by Heaven, the Japanese character for "dog" resembles the character for "Heaven." The English word "dog" is "god" when reversed. I now totally believe this story.

Incidentally, other domestic animals that are said to have followed include horses, sheep, cattle, and rabbits, which also do not have a part indicating animals in their Japanese characters. Animals that do have the characters with a part indicating animals, such as cats, raccoons, and wolves, are said to have been changed from dogs later on for some reason.

I find Japanese *kanji* fascinating. Through studying how each character is developed, we may be able to accurately identify the origin of each letter and perhaps therein solve many of today's remaining mysteries.

For example, the Japanese character for "darkness" symbolizes enclosing a sound inside a gate. This perfectly reflects a concept of quantum mechanics. No matter how small a thing may be, as long as it has energy, it gives off a sound. Darkness must have been perceived as the world with no sound.

A lexicon of Japanese *kanji* begins with indexes for the left-hand side, the right-hand side, and the top parts of characters. In terms of animals, the list includes only a limited number of parts, such as dog, cattle, sheep, insect, boar, shellfish, horse, fish, and bird. The Japanese character for each of the other animals has one of these portions, and the remaining part of the character is something that indicates that particular animal's characteristics.

I believe these animals that became the parts in *kanji* are the ones that were sent to earth first; later in the process of evolution, the other animals were created.

THE MYSTERIOUS LIFE OF PLANTS

A little more than thirty years ago an interesting book titled *The Secret Life of Plants* was published in the United States. It became a best seller in America, its German edition sold more than a hundred thousand copies, and in 1987 it was translated into Japanese. (Some of you may also remember the popular 1979 soundtrack Stevie Wonder composed for the film documentary based on the book.) I refer to this book because it includes a lot of data to support the idea that all life came from the universe. For example, plants respond to human consciousness, plants synchronize with certain people, and plants have personalities.

Some of the book's chapter titles are listed below, and we should seriously think about the book's contents and the results of the experiments described therein.*

- "Plants and ESP"

- "Plants Can Read Your Mind"

- "Plants That Open Doors"

- "Visitors from Space"

- "The Metamorphosis of Plants"

- "Plants Will Grow to Please You"

*In Japan, Akira Mikami actually put the concepts of the book into practice and wrote several highly respected books on this subject, including *Joint Research with Plants* and *Plants Warn Us*.

- "The Harmonic Life of Plants"

- "Plants and Electromagnetism"

- "Force Fields, Humans, and Plants"

- "The Mystery of Plant and Human Auras"

- "Soil: The Staff of Life"

- "Mind over Matter"

Many scientists started to pay attention to the unique informational abilities of plants, and now many of these once revolutionary ideas are commonly accepted as fact.

Unlike humans and animals, plants can't move. I don't think that plants feel stress about this fact. In terms of atomic compositions, I believe that plants are simpler beings than humans and animals.

Let's suppose one plant is made up of atoms A, B, C, D, and E, while another one is composed of B, E, F, G, and H. I have no doubt that plants have emotions, but I think different plants have different emotions.

The simpler atomic composition of a plant means its *hado* is purer and has stronger energy for

"RESPECT"
A person you respect is perhaps one who
has a lofty and generous heart.

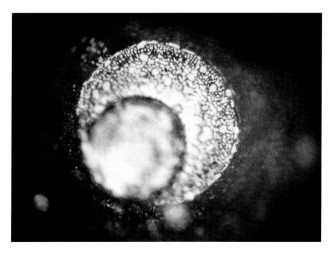

"NO GOOD"
Negative words, including forceful expressions
such as "Do it," can deny life in all its forms.
These words can prevent children from
growing freely and easily.

"CLEAN"
This crystal seems to indicate
that "clean" is one quality of a
person who does not exaggerate
his or her self-importance or
show off. "Clean" describes
someone who is honest.

"LOVE OF ONE'S NEIGHBORS"
"Neighbors both sides and three
across" is a common Japanese
expression. This crystal looks
more like "neighbors both sides
and six across." It is nice to have
good neighbors with whom you
can cooperate.

"PHILANTHROPY"
In the same way that philanthropy is felt to be universal,
knowing no limits, so too
this crystal grew out evenly,
reaching in all directions.

"LOVE OF HUMANITY"
As the crystal depicting "love of one's neighbors"
grows farther, it will become like this one.
The shape is closer to perfection.

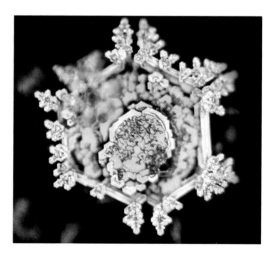

"BLIND LOVE"
Perhaps blind desperate love, in which one is
grasping at straws, or love that is based on wishful
thinking, is not true love. Here, with the center distorted,
water did not yield a beautiful crystal.

"LOVE AND THANKS"
Interestingly, no other crystals
formed after water was exposed
to words are more beautiful
than this one. This teaches us a
very important lesson.

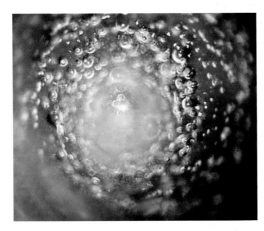

"I WILL KILL YOU"
The spiral in this
frightening crystal
resembles a snake
lying in a coil.

"HONESTY"
This crystal seems to indicate
past, present, and future.
The center, representing the
present, looks like a mirror
that reflects things as they are.

"FRIENDSHIP"

Can you help friends when they are in the midst of hardship? Doing so is not always easy, but imagine how good it would be if we could help them without hesitation.

"LOVE OF SELF"

A person cannot love others without first loving him- or herself.

"DO IT!"

It seems no life-form wants to be forced to do something. To live by one's own will is the essence of life.

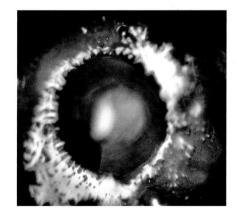

THE CHILDREN OF KITAKAWABE ELEMENTARY SCHOOL
Along with their families, the children of Kitakawabe Elementary School
drew water from a nearby reservoir. Then these thirty people made a
circle, clasped hands, and recited to the water: "Water, I love you."
"Water, I thank you." "Water, I respect you."

Top: Before prayerful recitation.

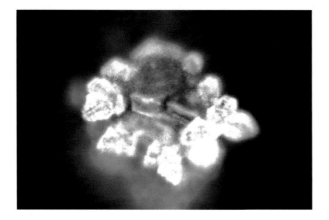

Bottom: After prayerful recitation.

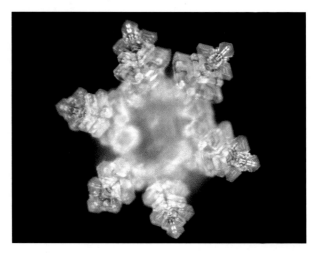

KIYOMASA WELL AT MEIJI SHRINE

Seeing a beautiful crystal like this one form in spring water from the middle of a city as large as Tokyo is rare. The water crystal shown here must be reflecting the devout prayers that men and women of all ages have offered while visiting this famous shrine.

THE SEA

Water that was exposed to "the sea" resulted in a crystal that rapidly grew into intricate shapes, in a way depicting the power of the changing sea of Nature itself.

SHOWING WATER "HADO"

All things are created by *hado* (vibration). The crystal here showed remarkable growth, almost as if it were making a large mandala.

"IMAGINE" BY JOHN LENNON
Playing this song resulted in a beautiful dreamy-looking
crystal that it is not connected at its center.
Perhaps "imagination" is something light and floating.

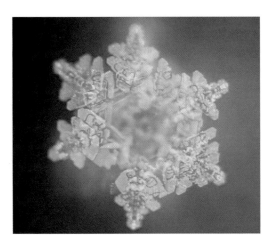

SENDING WORDS FROM ISRAEL TO TOKYO
The feeling of "love and gratitude" was sent from my seminar site
in Israel to the tap water in a Tokyo office. We all recited, "Water,
I love you. Water, I thank you. Water, I respect you." That message
reached across space and resulted in this beautiful crystal.

specific types of information. This may explain why plants have better communication abilities than humans and animals, and they can communicate with other plants on this planet as well as with the home base somewhere in the universe.

Due to excess stresses and pressures, we humans seem to have lost our ability to fully utilize our communication potentials, but I believe any of us can obtain necessary information through plants, as long as our intention is in accordance with the benevolence of the universe (love).

A STORY OF A PLANET

If humans, animals, and plants were sent here from the same star somewhere in the universe, the reasons and purposes must be the same for all beings.

The mission that all beings received must have been "to transform the wild earth into a friendly, peaceful, and plentiful planet." For this common purpose, I believe that the three parties were supposed to get along well and help one another. All beings were expected to live on earth by utilizing the soils and atoms that had been sent here in advance.

The first comers might have been heat-resistant plants—for example, ferns. The information came in the form of rain and arrived on the ground. It resonated with certain kinds of atoms and manifested as ferns that had green leaves, for example. Through photosynthesis, a special ability given to them, ferns were made to absorb carbon dioxide, which was abundant on the surface of the earth, and to produce oxygen.

Because of the advance party's efforts over tens of thousands of years, the earth's environment became gentler. During this time, the atoms needed for synthesizing certain animals must have been cultivated. The sender then encoded the information about animals, perhaps microorganisms at first, into water and launched them to earth.

Many more years later, the planet's environment finally became suitable for humans. All of the 108 atoms were on earth at that time, and the temperature averaged around 30°C. The seas, rivers, lakes, and ponds were in place. There was now ample oxygen thanks to plant presence over tens of thousands of years. Then humans came to the earth accompanied by domestic animals.

The arrival of humans and animals was also needed for plants, because in order for the plants, which required carbon dioxide to survive, to continue to produce oxygen, they needed the beings that consumed oxygen.

Thus the soil, which existed on the earth from the beginning; the water, which came from far away in the universe; and the oxygen produced by plants were all in place on this planet. The issue then became how to maintain the balance of the four parties (humans, animals, plants, and soil) under the leadership of humans.

Naturally, humans must have come full of gratitude for the other beings—soil, plants, animals, and water—that created the environment where they could also exist. However, for some reason, humans lessened their gratitude as time passed and came to think only about themselves.

As a result, there is something wrong at this time. Unless we humans reconsider our origins, worse things are yet to come. I believe we are now at a turning point where we must choose our future direction.

HUMANS HAVE INNATE GOODNESS

Some readers will undoubtedly view what I have just described as totally absurd. They may want to scold me, saying, "Outrageous! Don't talk non-sense!" Nevertheless, what I really wanted to convey is that most of us pay so little attention to our origins. I believe that we share a common desire to live humanely. If so, I believe it is important to continue our search for our origin and challenge ourselves to discover it.

As I said earlier, I initially thought we were the exiles of the universe. This was based on a view of human nature as fundamentally depraved. However, I changed my mind after the arrival of new theories, such as that about Indigo Children.* As I studied more about water through taking photographs of frozen water crystals, the new way of thinking became much clearer to me. I now have no doubt that we were sent here with missions and roles. It is a view of human nature as fundamentally good and is based on something I observed. No matter how polluted the lake or tap water looked initially, water responded to our thoughts and prayers. Even the water that previously produced only ugly crystals was able to form beautiful crystals when we sent it our pure thoughts and

---

*This is the name of a new type of children identified by Lee Carroll and Jan Tober in their 1999 book, *The Indigo Children*.

prayers. The beauty seemed to be a function of how pure our thoughts and prayers were.

I have observed this phenomenon in more than twenty cases and have included the results in my books: for example, the water at Fujiwara Dam after the prayer on the cover of the first volume of *Messages from Water*; the tap water of Tokyo after the children's prayer in the video version of the book; the water of Lake Picchu Cava in São Paulo, Brazil, after the prayer; and the water after five hundred *hado* instructors' simultaneous distant prayers.

These facts convinced me that all humans have innate goodness, because the water in the above circumstances was contaminated environmentally or by antiseptic chemicals and it would produce absolutely no crystal in normal circumstances, yet it created beautiful hexagons after the prayers. This reminded me of the Buddha's metaphor about lotus flowers.

As you know, lotuses grow in mud; however, they yield lovely blossoms. Using lotus flowers as a metaphor, the Buddha told us, "Even in the worst environment, people can still blossom beautifully."

As I have been saying, we are water. No matter how contaminated or dirty water may become, it can still form exquisite crystals reflecting people's beautiful thoughts and prayers. What this implies is that we humans, too, can open our lovely flowers even in adverse circumstances. By meeting with beautiful minds and receiving their help, we can transform as Jean Valjean does after meeting the bishop with a merciful heart.

In other words, even an evil man is intrinsically good at the subatomic level. I now deeply believe this. Humans are affected at the atomic or molecular level, just as the environment is polluted especially at the molecular level.

So, with what missions were we, as good beings, sent to earth? Before I get into this subject, I would like to share my perspective on God and religions.

DOES GOD EXIST?

Growing up, I didn't know much about God and religions. I was raised in a family with no religious practices. Moreover, I grew up in a city and didn't learn much about everyday Buddhist rituals, either.

One thing I remember is attending Sunday school (a traveling church) provided by the occupying forces right after World War II. I still remember some of the hymns I learned at that time. My motivation was the chocolate and cookies that I was given for attending the school.

So I never deeply thought about God. Even when I was a high school student naively discussing the big questions of life with my friends, we generally talked about philosophy, not about God and religions. It may be because of my attitude toward God and religions that the first twenty-five years of my working life were lacking God's blessings.

However, my attitude changed after I turned forty-five and became involved with *hado* and water. My thoughts particularly changed as I started *hado* consultations for those who suffered from diseases by using MRA, the *hado* measuring device, and transcribing the necessary information onto distilled water called "micro-clustered water." In ten years, I treated more than fifteen thousand people with *hado* water, and I got increasingly more accurate results as I gained more experience. During that time, I noticed that those who reflected upon themselves according to their religious teachings and deepened their understandings of the basics—love and gratitude—had a better improvement rate than those who didn't. Empirically, I came to realize that all diseases are derived from lack of love and gratitude at the DNA level, including karma from past lives. Thus I couldn't help but believe in the existence of the Divine.

I realized the following: Christ and Buddha were the sons of God. If a person strayed from their teachings, he or she would get sick. If the diseases turned very severe, the person would die. Death means the negation of being as a human. Therefore, as long as we want to live as human beings, we need to believe in the existence of the Divine and follow the teachings. The concept of God is love and gratitude.

From another perspective, I believe it is reasonable to assume the existence of the Divine.

"How was the universe—complex and subtle—created?" This is an eternal theme for humans to ponder. Perhaps it will remain an eternal question as long as we stay in the three-dimensional realm—as long as our soul stays in the physical body. Nonetheless, we shouldn't stop our quest for the answer, because I believe that our ultimate goal is to seek and find the answer. This is an exciting and interesting challenge. At the same time, answering this question will be more difficult than solving a complex mathematical equation. I tend to think that the answer will turn out to be very simple when we finally figure it out.

I certainly hope that we can get as close to the truth as possible. I imagine finding the answer in this three-dimensional world would be more profound and exciting than in the otherworld. Such an experience might be called a true pleasure.

When we work on a difficult mathematical equation, it is sometimes easier to proceed if we assume the answer and work back to see if it is correct.

In this case, the variable x in our equation is God. Dr. Kazuo Murakami, professor emeritus at the University of Tsukuba, uses the term "Something Great" instead. "God" is not just a term we should use in a religious sense; rather, I believe, it should be included in scientific terminology as well.

Some people dislike and feel embarrassed to use the term "God." "Authoritative" scientists tend to be found in this group. They tend to remain in their specialized fields, rather than coordinating with others holistically. In such an environment, it is impossible to reach the most important truth.

So, in order to find the answer, we shall assume that God exists. The Bible and the Sutras, which contain the teachings of Christ and Buddha, respectively, will be our reference books.

I am sure that there are other great religions as well, but my knowledge is superficial even with the Bible and the Sutras. Therefore, I rely on the realm of my subconscious, which I believe exists somewhere in my brain. I feel that the realm is now getting quite close to the surface and within my reach, more so than with most people.

I suppose my experience of *hado* measuring and consulting for more than fifteen thousand people contributed to bringing my subconscious to the surface, as I was able to help these people bring their subconscious memories up. Additionally, water taught me a lot after I acquired the technology of water crystal photography. I am especially blessed in this respect.

In the next section, I would like to share my hypothesis (or fairy tale?). If it's contradictory to the teachings of the Bible, the Sutras, or other religious writings, I would very much appreciate the input of clergy and other religious scholars.

WHERE DID THE WORD
COME FROM?

The Bible says that God created the universe in seven days. It also says, "In the beginning was the Word." I am not going to talk about the "seven days," but what does this reference to the Word mean?

For more than a decade, I conducted many experiments with water and took photographs of water crystals. The most amazing thing I observed about water was that when water was shown words, it responded positively to the positive words and negatively to the negative words. For example, water responded by forming beautiful crystals when it was exposed to "thank you." It responded horribly to "you fool." At first, I considered an experiment of talking to water. However, because of the great variance among people in talking, I adopted the method of typing a word on a sheet of paper and exposing it to water for one day and one night. Empirically, I had known that words had their own *hado* (vibrations).

The water's responses were the same when it was shown not only Japanese words but also words in other languages, such as English, German, Korean, and French. Naturally, many people who read my books or came to my seminars asked me why water responded in these ways. I usually explain it like this.

Since I was born in Japan and raised by Japanese-speaking parents, I speak Japanese fluently. If I were raised by a wolf, I would be speaking a wolf language, but not a single word in Japanese. The same is true for everybody.

For example, many people in Brazil have pure Japanese DNA. If their parents didn't teach them Japanese, they cannot speak Japanese. So the language is not in our DNA but something we learn after birth.

Then what about the first humans, let's say Adam and Eve? Who taught them words? Nature! They must have learned various vibrations and sounds from nature and started to imitate them to communicate with other humans. Great nature has all kinds of vibrations and sounds. For example, there are the roars of lions and tigers, which are dangerous to humans, and the calls of goats and rabbits, which have safe and gentle natures. Also, the sounds in nature include the murmur of streams and the rumbling of flooding water.

As humans accumulated many experiences

over a very long time, the function of the vocal cords developed proportionately. Thus humans gradually created words and increased their vocabulary.

With this line of thought, it is easier to understand why there are so many languages. It is because aspects of natural environments, such as temperature and humidity, differ depending on where people live. For example, the Japanese archipelago is long and narrow. The north end lies in the subarctic zone, and the south end is in the subtropical zone. It has four distinct seasons. Each season has a different climate. Thus I believe that Japanese has more kinds and greater numbers of words than most other languages.

On the other hand, in Siberia and Alaska the climates are cold, and the seasons don't vary very much. As a result, the natural environment tends to be more uniform than in a place like the Japanese archipelago. Therefore, I believe, the vocabulary of the languages developed in these regions is much smaller than that of Japanese. However, I have heard that Inuit has more than 170 words for ice. This is because there are many aspects of ice in the arctic. It also indicates that the words were developed from natural phenomena.

This essence of nature appears to be the same everywhere. In most countries, snakes are feared and detested, while almost all flowers are viewed as sweet and lovable. However, the difference in temperature and humidity influences frequencies. The climate in each region gives off a different frequency. Thus the difference in sounds resulted in the different names or words for the same plants or animals. For example, the sound of a pig is expressed "oink, oink" in English, but "boo, boo" in Japanese.

BEAUTIFUL WORDS CREATE BEAUTIFUL NATURE

As we analyze the development of languages, we realize an important concept about words. No matter what language it is, it is absolute. Words are not the result of random creations.

Of course, I am referring to the original languages that were developed when humans lived in nature. Their five senses must have been keen, as humans were at the mercy of nature, collected food in nature, and died in nature. Therefore, as discussed earlier, they must have made frantic efforts to feel the indications and *hado* of nature, and over a very long time they built the words as their vocal cords developed.

Naturally, when we pronounce *uchu* (cosmos) in Japanese, it must resonate with the vibration of the universe. When things have the same frequency, they resonate. In other words, they exchange energies. In this manner, they converse.

For our ancestors, the *hado* of the universe they felt in Japan was *uchu*. Similarly, the *hado* of the universe must have sounded like *kosmos* to the ancient Greeks, "cosmos" to the ancestors of the Anglo-Saxons. It is expressed as *cosmos* in French, *cosmo* in Italian, *cosmos* in Spanish, *cosmos* in Portuguese, *kosmos* in Dutch, *Kosmos* in German, *kocmoc* in Russian, *cosmos* in Latin, and *yuzhou* in Chinese.

The word for the universe in many of these languages is very similar. As the universe is vast and something to be felt by looking up, there might not have been so many regional influences regarding this word in different languages.

Let's consider water, a very common substance. The word for water in different languages is *eau* in French, *acqua* in Italian, *agua* in Spanish, *água* in Portuguese, *water* in Dutch, *Wasser* in German, *aqua* in Latin, and *shuy* in Chinese.

Anyway, Japanese has the word *kotodama* (the spirit of languages). *Kotodama* does not refer to the spirit world; rather, it is a science that can be explained by the theory of quantum vibration.

In my seminar, I usually summarize the discussion above by saying that it underlines the importance of using correct and positive words in our daily lives.

Words are *hado* (vibration).

Words are the products of nature.

Therefore, beautiful words create beautiful nature.

Dirty words create dirty nature.

This is the essence of the universe.

WHAT WATER IS TELLING US

When we go back to the origin and explore how words were developed, we can better understand the biblical phrase "In the beginning was the Word." I think that the Word was made by God and used by God. God must have thought to create a utopia on earth.

At first, several stars (seven stars)* were allotted to deliver the substances (atoms) to make the foundation of the earth in the form of meteorites. The meteorites collided with the earth, creating enormous energy that resulted in the formation of a large amount of magma at the core of the earth.

When the earth eventually became the size it is today, meteorites stopped flying in; but the earth was still a huge ball of fire and exploding gases. Observing the earth from high above, God created something and sent it to the earth to extinguish the fire and cool the heat down at just the right time. This was water. Every time God sent water to the earth, he gave water words and messages, which encoded his blueprint. Also, God designed water so as to store memories. Since the distance to the earth was great, God transformed water into ice, a more stable form, so that water could remember the messages. At this stage, God gave water the information about creating life later and the neces-

---

*More about this later.

sary wisdom for sustaining life in the form of vibrations, or words.

Right before water arrived on the earth, it woke up. It checked the entrusted messages that were in the form of crystals. Water crystals do not appear when the ice is very hard, that is, with a temperature lower than -15°C.

Upon its arrival on the earth, water worked on the atoms sent there in advance to create life phenomena. The base for the phenomena was hydrogen bonds, which enabled chemical reactions to take place.

According to God's plan, the first life-form was created. Now God decided to send his children with the basic concept of love and gratitude. What slipped God's mind was that he created the earth in three dimensions.

First, love was absolute; second, gratitude was relative; and the third thing needed was direction—for example, respect based on love and gratitude. This concept is founded on an ancient tradition in Japan—that of one, two, and three.

Of course, God noticed this missing element immediately and tried to add it to the basic design, but he had another idea. "It would not be so interesting to make everything perfect from the beginning. Let's keep the earth as it is now. I will watch in which direction my children lead the earth."

The humans who were sent to the earth in the form of water crystals were confused, as they didn't know which way to go. After struggles, they started to learn their direction from nature. It was a natural consequence, as they had to find food in nature and live in harmony with nature.

Humans were not equipped with weapons. They could not fly, did not have the destructive power of dinosaurs, and could not run fast like cheetahs. Moreover, humans had neither sharp fangs like lions and tigers nor the ability to live in water like fish. What humans could do was limited to sharpening their five senses and using their wisdom. So they did.

. . .

The most reliable human sense was hearing. Humans listened carefully to the vibrations/sounds that nature gave off and learned which were safe and which weren't. When it was safe, they went out and looked for food. When it wasn't, they hid inside caves. They soon learned that it was more efficient to work together as a group than to work alone. Thus they formed a community, an extension of their families.

To communicate with one another, they first used hand signs. However, the signs were not effective unless they were displayed within a visible distance. Next, they imitated and vocalized the sounds in nature. As their vocal cords developed over a very long time, they created words. In the beginning, the words were the copies of the vibrations/sounds in nature. The words created from great nature were themselves the words of God. Through great nature, I believe humans acquired the words of God. Thus they acquired the ability to converse with God.

OUR HOME STAR

Where does God reside?

Assuming that we are the children of God, I would think that God resides at the center of the universe. Although it is arguable where the center is, I would go with the thought of the North Star as the center.

One thing that puzzles me is that although the location of the North Star remains unchanged, it is said that the star has a cycle of twenty-six thousand years and is replaced by other stars.

Five thousand years ago the North Star was Thuban; in twenty-five hundred years it will be Errai in Cepheus; ten thousand years later it will be Deneb in Cygnus; thirteen thousand years later, it will be Vega in Lyra; and Polaris, currently in the Little Dipper, is expected to return as the North Star in twenty-six thousand years.

What should we make of this? Is it possible that God is on a rotation or shift system? I will save the exploration of these questions until later; for now let's think about where we came from.

I believe we came from the Big Dipper, which may sound startling; but the reason may be explained by my special attachment to the number 7.

Why do we have the seven basic notes? (sound)

Why does a rainbow have seven colors? (color)

Why are there seven days in a week? (time)

Why do we have the seven chakras in our bodies? (body)

I am sure you can think of many other examples associated with 7. For instance, we have many expressions in Japanese with the number 7, including lucky seven, the seven spring herbs, the seventh day after death ceremony, the forty-ninth (the square of 7) day after death ceremony, the seventh evening Star Festival (the seventh day of the seventh month), the seven downs and eight ups, seven lights, seven gods, seven misfortunes, seven changes, and seven mysteries. No doubt there are many mysterious expressions related to 7 in other languages as well. I am fascinated by the fact that the important elements for humans (sound, color, time, and body) are related to the number 7.

So when a friend of mine and I were talking about our origin, he said it must be the Big Dipper, seven stars. I was immediately convinced.

. . .

The Japanese character for "star" has two components—"day" and "coming into life." There must be a relationship between a birthday and the home star. By understanding the relationship between our home star and the Big Dipper, we may be able to get closer to knowing whether this concept is correct.

As I've discussed previously, I believe that *kanji* contain very reliable information and that when we understand their meaning we can solve quite a few of our mysteries. When I reflect on *kanji*, I am convinced that ancient humans were able to solve the mysteries of the universe to a certain degree. This seems especially true when we consider that modern science has a history of approximately 150 years and that the ancient wisdom was developed over tens of thousands of years of human culture.

It may not be true of all ancient wisdom, of course, but the wisdom of Thales, Aristotle, and Plato, for example, is still highly respected today. They discovered the truth that underlies today's humanity more than two thousand years ago. Even the use of astrology to forecast a person's character and destiny has been common for more than five thousand years. Astrology does not show any sign of decline; rather, it seems to gain more popularity as it is taken up daily by TV programs and such. In general, the way of thinking and the customs that have lasted more than three thousand years are mostly dependable. Humans must not have been so shortsighted.

Five

THE
POWER
OF
PRAYER

PEOPLE'S THOUGHTS ARE
TRANSMITTED TO WATER

Our consciousness affects water. Our collective
thoughts have an especially remarkable effect. They
are like laser light that can reach even the surface
of the moon. The following story is a miracle of
water purification at Fujiwara Dam.

In late August 1997, I went to speak at the Ko-
gakukan Hall of the Omi Jingu shrine at the invi-
tation of the Lake Biwa Research Institute, a civic
organization. The title of my talk was "Hado, Water, and Life."

There, I met Kato Hoki, an ascetic priest of
Shingon Tantric Buddhism. He was the chief

priest at a temple in the city of Omiya. As if he had been waiting for me, he showed me two photographs. They looked like featureless scenic views of a lake, taken from the same place and from the same angle.

While showing me the pictures, Reverend Kato said to me, "These pictures were taken at the lakeside of Fujiwara Dam, Gunma Prefecture, on the same day. I have been practicing the religious asceticism of Shingon Tantric Buddhism for many years. As I was practicing, I noticed that my incantations and prayers seemed to result in purifying the water around me.

"So a few months ago, I went to the lake and performed the incantations and prayers for water purification for about one hour. There was a noticeable difference in water clarity before and after."

When I looked at the pictures more intently, I noticed an obvious difference. The lake water in the picture taken after the prayer looked much clearer.

"Wow! It's amazing! It's really amazing! But I can understand this, Reverend Kato. It is because of *hado* and the spirit of languages, isn't it?"

"Indeed, it is. My temple practices Shingon

Tantric Buddhism. 'Shingon' means exactly 'to convey the spirit of languages.'"

"Reverend, would you please take me to the site next time? By taking water crystal photographs before and after your ascetic practice, I believe we can confirm the difference more clearly."

"Of course! I will let you know when the date is set."

One and a half months later, Reverend Kato and I went to Fujiwara Dam accompanied by Mr. Sato and Mr. Mochizuki, who were in charge of water crystal pictures and videotaping. There was another person with us, K., who miraculously recovered from terminal cancer after Reverend Kato performed his incantations and prayers.

WORD ENERGIES

Fujiwara Dam seemed stagnant and gloomy. This man-made lake is not really a lake but a huge reservoir. The reservoir at Fujiwara Dam seemed to have the same problem as any other dam in Japan. Since there was almost no convection current, accelerated oxidation was adversely affecting the surrounding natural environment. No beautiful autumn colors were reflected on the water's surface.

Reverend Kato chose a site and prepared for his ascetic practice. He put a branch of a *sakaki* plant at each of the four corners of the site and purified it with sake he had brought. Once the sacred space was created and purified, no one but the ascetic priest was allowed to be inside.

Slowly and solemnly, the priest started his practice. His rich and ringing voice gave no indication that he was seventy-two years old. With his fingers, he made various hand signs, and from time to time he shouted out briskly and loudly.

I noticed that his voice and the hand signs were directed not to the reservoir but to two glasses of water on a stand at his feet.

Immediately, I understood what he was doing. Perhaps he designated one glass of water as yang and the other as yin. By concentrating all his energy into the yin and yang waters, he was influencing the water in the reservoir through resonance. Thus the resonance effect started by the water in the glasses would give lively vibrations to the reservoir.

.   .   .

Reverend Kato's incantations and prayers lasted about one hour without a break, and his ascetic practice came to an end. I felt awed and deeply moved by watching the priest's solemn, whole-hearted devotion. After a while, I said to him, "Reverend Kato, thank you very much. If you don't mind, I wish to ask you some questions about your practice." Like a professional interviewer, I held a microphone for our videotaping and asked many questions. Reverend Kato was not at all out of breath and humbly answered my questions. After about fifteen minutes of interviewing, Mr. Sato suddenly screamed, "Mr. Emoto, look at the lake! The water is clearing up rapidly. It is really amazing!"

Mr. Mochizuki also exclaimed, "Wow! Really great! It is so clear now that we can see the trees reflecting on the water. That reflection wasn't there before."

I turned my head toward the water, and I was stunned. A gentle breeze had now stopped; the ripples on the water were gone, too. The water surface was like a mirror reflecting the surrounding colorful scenery.

"Look, Reverend Kato. It's incredible, isn't it? When we came here, the lake surface had almost no reflection. It is so beautiful now. It's really great! I am awestruck."

Without showing any excitement, Reverend Kato smiled calmly and said, "Indeed. It is getting quite clear."

I thought to myself, "Well, I didn't expect it to be this great." Then I said to him, "Actually, I thought that if we took the samples of water before and after the prayer and took crystal photographs, we might be able to detect the difference, but it is so obvious to our own naked eyes that we do not need to do this to see what's changed. It is awesome. As I expected, the energy of the spirit of languages is verifiable. Thank you very much."

THE SECRET OF THE HEPTAGON WATER CRYSTAL

Three days later, my excitement grew even more, reaching a peak when Mr. Sato handed me the crystal pictures of the lake water samples taken before and after Reverend Kato's incantations and prayers. With trembling voice, he said, "President, tremendous things have happened!" Normally he would have addressed me as "Chief," but then he excitedly used "President."

The photographs he handed me were indeed beyond my imagination. The water crystal picture before the prayer was horrible. Examined more closely, it looked like a woman struggling and suffering in despair. However, the other picture turned out to be beautiful. To my amazement, it was not a hexagon but a heptagon. We have never been able to take such a picture of a heptagonal crystal before. I wondered why this happened; soon I came to realize the reasons and developed a new hypothesis: Water is a pilot for all beings. When humans, who reside in the three-dimensional world, move to the otherworld, water alone can synchronize with the energy levels of their consciousness. Water is the only agent that does not interfere with humans and takes them to the other dimensions as they are. Therefore, in the three-dimensional world, water must change its physical properties variously; thus, it gives us hints for its functions. The ultimate aspiration of water in the solar system must be "light" itself.

In other words, we are originally the children

of light. Our goal for the moment is to go back to that status.

The heptagonal water crystal taught me this new hypothesis. This thought touched my heart and moved me almost to tears. It was a real honor and pleasure to meet with the Reverend Kato Hoki.

This experience led me to come up with a quixotic plan—purifying the water of Lake Biwa with the spirit of languages. This plan was carried out on July 25, 1999, and resulted in a wonderful phenomenon.

A month after the Fujiwara Dam experience, Mr. Sato called K., who had accompanied Reverend Kato and had subsequently heard dreadful news.

He communicated that a week after we went to Fujiwara Dam, the local TV station reported that a young woman's body had surfaced at the reservoir there. The next day, the murderer of the woman was arrested. I don't believe this is just a coincidence.

The water crystal picture before the prayer had indeed looked like the distorted face of a woman who was suffering. On the other hand, in the heptagonal crystal picture, I saw a merciful face like that of Mahatma Gandhi.

. . .

This experience was very shocking. Since then, I have come to recognize the spiritual world and the spirit of languages. It feels uplifting and invigorating for me to think that the energy from the spirit of languages can influence all life-forms on earth. When it is based on true love and gratitude, the spirit generates unbelievably refined energy to affect all life on Gaia.

FROM ISRAEL TO TOKYO—
BEYOND TIME AND SPACE

The first time I really prayed was more than thirty years ago, in front of a TV set. It was being reported that the *Apollo 13* spacecraft had had a serious explosion in one of its oxygen tanks while en route to the moon, and images of people all over the world praying for the three astronauts' safe return were being broadcast.

One of the scenes that stuck in my memory was

of Jewish people praying earnestly at the Wailing Wall. Following these people, I also prayed for the astronauts' safe return in my own way.

It might have been the first time that collective prayers had occurred worldwide, transcending races and religions. It must have been the power of these prayers that enabled the astronauts' miraculous return despite the one-in-three-million odds.

That experience of more than thirty years ago is one of the driving forces behind my promotion of international activities with prayer as the theme, although I had previously been indifferent to religions and religious education.

In July 2003, I visited Israel. Declaring July 25 as the day to offer our love and gratitude to all the water on earth, I visited the Jordan River to pray for world peace. There I decided to do a completely unexpected experiment.

My unscheduled experiment was to send love and gratitude from the seminar site near Lake Galilee to the tap water placed on my desk in my office in Asakusabashi, Tokyo. I truly wanted to see how water crystals would change before and after the participants offered spoken prayers. Having had all the participants readily consent, I showed a slide picture of the glass of water on the desk in my office.

To the water, we recited and sent our words, "Water, I love you." "Water, I thank you." "Water, I respect you." We repeated these phrases three times. That's all the experiment involved.

I promised the audience I would show the result in five hours. Mr. Kizu, a researcher, was on standby in the laboratory in Tokyo; at midnight I sent him an e-mail to freeze the water. Shortly after, his e-mail response arrived: "I have just finished the preparation. I will be able to send you the result in three hours." It was 2:00 a.m. in Japan; 8:00 p.m. in Israel.

The time had come to show the participants the result. It was about 11:00 p.m. I said to the audience, "I have just received the picture that resulted from your cooperation. Let me show it to you."

Did the *hado* energy in the prayer and words of love and gratitude reach Tokyo more than twenty thousand kilometers away?

A beautiful water crystal appeared, although tap water in Tokyo had never formed crystals before. This is evidence of the power of prayer.

All things begin with consciousness. The world is made up of the consciousness of each and every one of us. If the earth is filled with the *hado* of ample love and gratitude, the world will manifest itself as love and gratitude.

A PRAYER

When we were children,
No one taught us the importance of a prayer.
Not our mothers, fathers, grandmothers, grandfathers,
Nor schoolteachers.
During the war, they all must have prayed.
But they thought that the prayer was not heard,
Because they had atomic bombs, burned houses, loss of loved
*   ones.*
So I, too, didn't pray until I was in my mid-fifties.
Well, when I was small, I did go to the Sunday school of the
*   occupying forces and I prayed, "Jesus, Jesus, please*
*   make me a good child of yours,"*
Since I knew I could get chocolate and sweets.
But after working with water for fifteen years,
I was taught.
"It was wrong. Prayers are really important."
What was wrong was how they prayed.

POWER
OF
PRAYER

123

They prayed for winning the war.
They prayed for good fighting of their husbands, sons,
*   fathers, and brothers.*
Prayers then were forced, too.

A prayer for destruction will never be heard,
Because water is a messenger.
Water carries only the prayers with love and gratitude.
This is proven by water crystals.
When we pray for our families' safety,
When we pray for our loved ones' health,
Our prayer is heard.
For us, all the people on the earth are important,
Because all of us are a family living on the earth.
So let's pray together for the peace of our family.
Let's pray for peace on earth.
Our prayer will surely be heard!

Six

TUNE
IN TO
THE
VIBRATION
OF
LOVE

THE ETERNAL THEMES OF
HUMAN BEINGS

As discussed earlier, the most difficult questions that we need to find the answers to are: Where did we come from? Why are we here? Where will we go after we die? Nobody would disagree about that. In this book I have described my attempt to find the answers to these questions.

Has it been several million years since human beings came into existence? The recorded history of humanity goes back a few thousand years. Throughout human history, the teachings of philosophers such as Plato, Socrates, Chuang-tzu, and Lao-tzu and of religious beings such as Christ and Buddha have offered signposts for solving these seemingly eternal mysteries. Although their teachings were expressed differently, they have all been respected as truth.

People today have difficulty believing unconditionally in the aspects of this world that exist only as mental or spiritual phenomena. People have a tendency to resist grasping the world in its entirety, and instead pick and choose the part of the teachings relevant to their own conditions and interpret that part according to their own needs. Contemporary tensions among religions, philosophies, and races seem to derive from these tendencies.

Fortunately or unfortunately (depending on how you look at it), I lacked a basic knowledge of religion and philosophy. On many occasions, I was faced with an important situation where I had to make a choice. Relying on my ethics and empathy, backed by the sense of justice that was growing inside me, I was able to make decisions and to live for more than sixty years without devoting myself to a specific religion or philosophy.

I am grateful for the happiness I feel in challenging myself to explore these questions at this stage of my life.

On the journey to reach this point, I had a fateful encounter with *hado* and water many years ago and success in taking water crystal pictures starting a few years later, and I've accumulated many photographs since then. These experiences have taught me how to paint freely; the canvas was Masaru Emoto, myself, and it was white in terms of philosophical and religious background.

The painting style was representational, not abstract. Namely, it was a scientific method of taking photographs with microscope cameras. My work was immediately recognized by twenty-first-century leaders in healing and spirituality. It played a role in proving and endorsing what they had accomplished. These leaders then spread news of my work worldwide. In time my work was affirmed by those who had a faithful religious belief in the sincere pursuit of a life purpose.

Eventually, my work was supported by many women intuitively, rather than logically. They were the ones who gave birth to babies after carrying fetuses for 280 days, babies that began as tiny fertilized eggs of almost 100 percent water and became small humans with tens of trillions of cells. They were the ones who had DNA for such life bearing. After receiving great resonance worldwide, I am no longer just an ordinary man in his sixties. With this realization, I ventured on a quest for answers to human beings' three eternal questions.

Let me summarize my working answers.

WHY DO WE HAVE THE ABILITY TO THINK?

Let me repeat: All life-forms cannot be born without water. Water was not intrinsic to this earth. It came from outer space, plunging through the earth's atmosphere in the form of ice in comets, which are still arriving. At this point, I am not going to discuss my views about what this phenomenon entails; I may be able to do so sometime in the future. Here it is sufficient to say:

1. Without water, no life has its birth.

2. Water came from the universe.

3. Therefore, all life, including humans, came from outer space.

The question then is: From where in the universe did we come? As discussed, I believe it to be

TUNE IN
TO THE
VIBRATION
OF
LOVE

the Big Dipper. Of course, this belief is just the result of my own reasoning. I hope readers will contemplate where our true home is by relying on their own sensibilities.

Honestly, I am not familiar with astrology, *bagua* divination, Chinese astrology, or numerology. Among old fortune-telling practices, I believe we can find the keys to discover where our true home is. Combining our knowledge and wisdom and generating ideas together, we will be able to hit upon key words for such a discovery.

Wherever our true home may be, I feel confident about how we were sent here because of what I have learned from photographs of water crystals. I have seen a great many of these pictures and eventually came to realize that water is the blueprint of reality.

Let's take a look at the pictures in Figures 16–18. The top photograph was taken after exposing water to a picture of the Izumo shrine, the middle to a view of cherry blossoms, and the bottom to an image of an elephant. Please take another, closer look; you will notice the similarity between the shapes of water crystals and the shapes of actual items. If water is shown the picture of a person's face, I am sure it will form a crystal by capturing his or her characteristic

Figures 16–18. After water was exposed to the picture of the Izumo shrine, the shrine's sacred straw rope appeared. There was a pink color in the center of the one exposed to the image of cherry blossoms, and a trunk in the crystal shown the picture of an elephant.

features. The foundation of my belief is derived from studying water crystals and conducting tuning-fork experiments. As I mentioned earlier, the most beautiful crystal was formed after water was exposed to "love and thanks."

A water crystal may be showing us a mandala of vibration or a design of life phenomena. If so, then the fundamental concept of this planet called Gaia is love and gratitude. In other words, the earth was originally designed with the concept of love and gratitude. Humans are entrusted to maintain that concept. The act of love gives every being vitality. Giving vitality is the same thing as giving vibration. As seen in tuning-fork experiments, in order for us to give off vibrations, we have to vibrate first. That is an ability given to us humans. Why? The reason is that only we humans can freely sing "do, re, mi, fa, sol, la, ti, do." No other being can sing songs in the same way we humans can.

In other words, only humans can freely modulate the source of energy—vibration—and then send it off. This ability at freely modulating vibration also explains our ability to think. Why can humans, unlike other animals, think? I believe it is because humans have the ability to freely modulate and transmit vibrational information. This ability has manifested itself as our wisdom, history, and civilization.

There are numerous and elaborate kinds of vibrations. Evidence can be seen in the fact that no two snowflakes are identical despite countless snowfalls since ancient times.

When we come up with grand ideas, they often arrive with what's described as a "flash" or "shock." These expressions also point out that humans have numerous and elaborate vibrations. I believe this is because of the variety of atoms that make up human beings. In other words, I believe that humans are made up using all of the atoms in the world. Let me cite my explanation for that from my book *Hado Jidai eno Jyomaku* (The Prelude to the *Hado* Age).

ALL THINGS HAVE MENTAL VIBRATIONS

I feel I have come to the place where I was supposed to come. Once, when I measured the *hado* of a cut flower, it indicated the emotion of sadness, which was previously thought to be something only humans could feel. From this experience, I developed the following hypothesis:

Be it negative mental *hado* such as frustration, anxiety, worry, and anger or positive *hado* such as sympathy, trust, kindness, and confidence, when humans have these mental vibrations *(hado),* they are expressed as such emotions.

These vibrations are actually common to all beings. Perhaps not only humans but also all things, including plants and minerals, share these emotions. To put it most generally: the *hado* energy that is the source of all phenomena is derived from the mental (conscious) *hado.*

Based on this hypothesis, I have conducted experiments on various materials, including diamonds, drugs, food, water, and ceramics. The results all support my hypothesis.

All the materials tested displayed the same emotions as humans do. This finding led me to another daring idea. However, before getting into it, I have one more finding to share.

GRUDGE AND GRATITUDE
HAVE THE SAME *HADO*

Once I was invited to speak at the Intuition Study Group (led by Mr. Yukio Funai of Funai

Consulting), and since Dr. Ronald Weinstock, the developer of MRA, happened to be in Japan at that time, I made arrangements for him also to speak at the seminar. He told me the following story during our preparation meeting for the seminar: "Hado has two aspects—positive and negative. Within one *hado* [vibration], there are positive and negative, and they are expressed in two extremes. For example, paired feelings such as grudge and gratitude, anger and kindness, and sadness and joy share their *hado*. Depending on a given person's positive or negative field, the same *hado* can be expressed quite oppositely."

I admired his explanation, because I had seen many cases that endorsed his point. You may want to think about your own personality in this context; you will probably find that you, too, have these contradictions and dualities.

ONE HUNDRED AND EIGHT WORLDLY DESIRES AND ELEMENTS

My idea grew and grew, and reached its climax when I referred to the *Japanese Dictionary of Physics and*

Chemistry and read about elements. The following was what I found:

> Proposed by Boyle in the late seventeenth century, Lavoisier in the latter half of the eighteenth century, and others, elements became recognized with experimental bases. The number of elements discovered was about thirty then. Subsequently, many more elements were discovered as new metals were found and spectroscopic analysis and X-ray spectroscopic analysis came into use.
>
> Next, new elements were discovered through nuclear reaction. Currently, 103 elements have been confirmed, from hydrogen, atomic number 1, to lawrencium, atomic number 103. Furthermore, an additional 5 new elements, from atomic numbers 104 through 109, excluding 108, were found through nuclear reaction.

When I saw that the total number of elements is 108, something flashed into my mind; I thought of the "108 worldly desires" that humans are said to have.

A SIGNPOST FOR NEW SCIENCE

Through the process described above, I developed another hypothesis: Each and every element that makes up all substances—humans, animals, and plants—has both positive (yang) and negative (yin) *hado*. Humans are made up of combinations of all 108 elements—the 103 elements in the periodic table and the 5 new elements. Other animals, plants, and substances have fewer elements.

For example, roses may be made up of combinations of thirty atoms. A joke goes, "A monkey is a human with three fewer hairs." Well, it may not be a joke after all; it may be implying that monkeys are made up of 105 elements, three fewer than humans.

Each element must have its intrinsic meaning in terms of *hado*. By analyzing elements using *hado* measuring devices such as MRA, we may be able to uncover the mysteries of humans and ultimately the mysteries of the universe. My intuition tells me hydrogen has the role of "information," oxygen that of "energy," and carbon that of "intelligence." I believe that each of the 108 elements has its own intrinsic role.

The concept of two fields, yin and yang, or

negative and positive, is the basic physical phenomenon in the universe, where condensation occurs through repeated attraction and repellency. When opposite fields collapse, everything loses stability and also collapses.

I am a little concerned that the newest among the 108 elements were discovered through nuclear reaction. I am anxious about whether the additional elements will disturb the balance of the universe.

In any event, I believe it is correct to say that the atoms that constitute the human body give rise to negative mental *hado*. In this vein, it is very important to eat the right foods. Foods are the only means by which our bodies are supplied with the necessary nutrients.

WHAT FOODS ARE
TRULY GOOD FOR US?

As you know, the human body consists of as many as sixty trillion cells. Each cell has minutely different vibrations. To vibrate, cells need to resonate with something else—foods.

Because the cells of both our bodies and foods

are made up of atoms, they share the same materials, and may therefore be said to be of the same sort. Naturally, the cells of our bodies want to live continuously according to the order of our DNA or our will. In other words, they want to continue vibrating. As discussed earlier, a cell cannot continue to vibrate by itself. So it gives off an SOS signal saying, "Give me vibration." It is the signal "I am hungry."

Attending to the signals of our cells, we relieve them by eating, sending them food. Since each cell is very small, the food is made into tiny, even microscopic parts through the digestive process. Water, of course, is always there to escort the foods so that they can move smoothly during the entire progression.

Ultimately, foods become the different frequencies that the various cells need. Through resonance phenomena, vibrational energies are distributed according to cells' needs, and they are revitalized again.

When we think about the relationship between foods and our cells, it becomes clear that the purer this symbiotic relationship is, the more efficiently energy exchange occurs. So foods that have frequencies that are very close to those of our cells are good for us.

Since we have sixty trillion cells, with many different needs, the best solution is a balanced diet with a wide variety of foods. In terms of energy, problematic foods are the ones with frequencies that are altered artificially, such as foods grown using chemical fertilizers and pesticides, foods containing artificial preservatives, and foods made with MSG.

When these foods are ingested constantly, our cells' physical properties will be altered, and this may trigger the development of cancers, incurable diseases, and mental disturbances. Suppose a cell gives off a certain signal when it gets weak. Then that cell can pick up a vibration that is similar but not exactly the same. This would inevitably result in the cell's properties being altered.

If you agree with what I have discussed in this section, I encourage you, especially if you are in a medical field or the food industry, to start studying vibrational nutrition. In the near future, I anticipate that technology will be developed to accurately measure the frequencies of each organ and each food.

TUNING IN TO THE *HADO* OF LOVE

When I wrote *Hado Jidai eno Jyomaku* (The Prelude to the *Hado* Age), I had yet to think of everything in terms of vibration. Currently, I view us humans as being equipped with many varieties of vibrations— that is, information—from our birth. I believe this is true because, as discussed earlier, every element has its intrinsic frequency, and our being made up of many elements gives us the ability to tune in to many different things.

For example, we can talk to beautiful flowers in the garden and cheer them up. Among the wild plants, we can find herbs and some plants that are edible. We are also good at tuning in to the frequencies of dogs and cats. Wherever we go, we can see people using a similar tone of voice to amuse babies.

Instinctively, we humans have the ability to tune in to others' frequencies. I believe this is possible because we share the same elements with them; we have their frequencies within ourselves.

We can directly give off vibrational energy that resonates with others, thereby revitalizing them. That energy is *love.* The recipient of the energy sends off a pleasure energy in return. That energy is *gratitude*. In this manner, love and gratitude complement each other and generate energy efficiently. This is exactly the source of free energy.

Science should have stayed focused on an extension of this concept of love and gratitude, yet something went wrong somewhere, and this principle was forgotten.

Worldly desires came into play: the ambition for fame, material greed, hunger for power, jealousy, fear of death, and so on. With these desires interfering, it was difficult to generate free energy. We can easily develop destructive energies in the short run, but we have a hard time developing love-and-gratitude energy or renewable energies in the long run.

How did this happen? I believe it resulted from having people in power at different times who wanted control over society. They successfully utilized the negative vibrations of people's worldly desires.

There is no value in denying our past. Perhaps we should accept it as the course that we had no choice but to take, because denying our past is tantamount to denying our existence. What we need to do is learn from the past and create the present and the future in a more hopeful way.

Returning to that important question, "Why are we here?," I share the following:

The role of humans is simply to give the vibration of love. As a natural consequence, the energy of gratitude will be generated. Thus the world will be balanced beautifully with these complementary energies.

Such energy is free, and it can continue forever, without drying up. The source of energy is water, H_2O. *H* represents gratitude, and *O* love. With one portion of *love* vibration and two portions of *gratitude,* energy will be created. Water is forever.

SOMETHING THAT CONTINUES FOREVER

We are water. We are vibration protected in water. The vibration collects atoms that were sent to the earth in advance and makes temporary "clothing" for us to wear. That clothing is our body. How we wear this clothing—with or without care—makes a difference in terms of how long it will last, and so life span differs from person to person.

Another factor that affects our life span is the *hado* inherited from our ancestors. When our ancestors left unfinished many things that they had wished to do, negative genes were created, and the size of our atomic clothing was disturbed to a degree determined by these unfinished desires. This disturbance may result in a shorter life span. But when we feel love and gratitude, our clothes will be easily mended. The clothes will also be repaired when we complete our ancestors' unfinished jobs.

When we take off our temporary clothes (death), what will happen? I believe there are two paths: one is to cross the river Styx and go to the otherworld; the other is to go through the cycle of reincarnation. Those who cross the Styx will become a part of water recirculation in the universe, and they will be sent to the next destination. Through the water circulation in the universe, the order of life in other stars will be maintained. Wherever we go, humans exist like the sun, giving the energy of love unstintingly.

Those who cannot cross the Styx are flunked students in this earthly school that trains humans to be peacekeepers in the cosmos. They must repeat the schooling until they can graduate. In our time there are so many repeaters that it is difficult to get back into school again.

To sum up: Passing or failing the earthly school depends on how much we can feel and exercise love and gratitude at the level of the body, not just in the head. We humans are supposed to vibrate. Our being is our soul in temporary clothing made up of atoms. In other words, we are vibrating souls. We cannot continue to vibrate alone. Unless we receive resonating vibrations from others, we stop vibrating—that is, we truly *die*.

Conversely, as long as we have resonating vibrations, our vibrations will not stop; thus there is no death. The absolute condition for receiving resonating vibrations from others is *gratitude*. In other words, as long as our bodies have feelings of love and gratitude, our life—vibration/soul—will never disappear and will be eternal.

EPILOGUE

This book is my attempt to explain plainly the true meanings of love and gratitude that I learned from my study of frozen water crystal pictures.

In the series of experiments in which words were shown to water to see the changes in crystal formation, the most beautiful crystal resulted from exposing water to the words "love and thanks." A label with the words "love and thanks" was pasted on a water bottle and left there for twenty-four hours. The picture was taken thirteen years ago, and I have not seen a more beautiful crystal since.

I have been pondering why such a beautiful water crystal was formed after showing the water "love and thanks." I finally found my answer. Once I had it, I felt that I needed to share my findings with my readers. Meanwhile, the Tokuma Shoten Publishing Company had asked me to write a book; so I took the opportunity to satisfy both goals. It was a struggle for me. With a title such as *The Shape of Love,* I needed a suitable structure and writing style. In the past, people tended to think of me as "Emoto, the Hard-Liner." Therefore, I had trouble changing my style. With Ms. Toyoshima's support and advice, I managed to work up my thoughts into a book. Having just finished reading the final galley proof that Ms. Toyoshima sent me, I realize once again how difficult it is to write this kind of book. What I have written is new science, with the added burden of trying to present *hado* in an easy-to-understand manner. Since *hado* is invisible, I needed a miracle.

The other tool I used to explain *hado* was the tuning fork and its sound. Sound clearly is also invisible, which is why I needed illustrations to explain tuning-fork experiments. It was virtually impossible to convey sound resonance or echo phenomena with enough presence that readers would feel as if they were listening.

As a writer, I still have to keep training myself to write correctly, as I wish to tell the important truth to as many people as possible. It is hard work, but I intend to enjoy it at the same time.

Well, what did you think of the book? Was it easy to read? What else? Your honest feedback will be very much appreciated. Please send your comments to my Web site: www.hado.net.

In closing, I must confess one thing. While writing this book, I became very ill and was almost hospitalized. I still have a lingering cold. I often talk about the importance of love and gratitude and say that the best way to avoid illness is to feel love and gratitude, yet I myself became sick. Why? It is because my heart is not filled with love and gratitude. I understand the concept in my head, but my love and gratitude are not substantial enough to reach the core of my body. No wonder it took six years for me to understand the message of love and gratitude from water.

.   .   .

I pledge that I will put love and gratitude into practice, together with you. As my first step, I dedicate this book to my beloved wife with gratitude.